DATE DUE

DEC 1 3 2009			
AP 12 '10			
NOV 2 1 2011			
APR 2 3 2014			

GENES & DISEASE

HUNTINGTON'S DISEASE

GENES & DISEASE

GENES & DISEASE

HUNTINGTON'S DISEASE

David M. Lawrence

CHELSEA HOUSE
PUBLISHERS

An imprint of Infobase Publishing

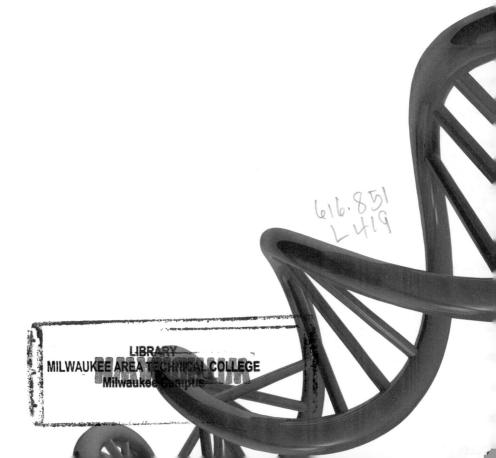

Chelsea House
An imprint of Infobase Publishing
132 West 31st Street
New York, NY 10001

Library of Congress Cataloging-in-Publication Data

Lawrence, David M., 1961–
   Huntington's disease / David M. Lawrence.
     p. cm. — (Genes and disease)
   Includes bibliographical references and index.
   ISBN 978-0-7910-9586-7 (hardcover)
   1. Huntington's chorea—Juvenile literature. I. Title. II. Series.
   RC394.H85L39 2009
   616.8'51—dc22   2009002039

Chelsea House books are available at special discounts when purchased in bulk quantities for businesses, associations, institutions, or sales promotions. Please call our Special Sales Department in New York at (212) 967–8800 or (800) 322–8755.

You can find Chelsea House on the World Wide Web at
http://www.chelseahouse.com.

Text Design by Annie O'Donnell
Cover Design by Ben Peterson

Printed in the United States of America

Bang NMSG 10 9 8 7 6 5 4 3 2 1

This book is printed on acid-free paper.

All links and Web addresses were checked and verified to be correct at the time of publication. Because of the dynamic nature of the Web, some addresses and links may have changed since publication and may no longer be valid.

CONTENTS

1

FADING AWAY

Woody Guthrie escaped the Dust Bowl of the 1930s to become one of the most important musicians ever to hail from the United States. The folk singer's vast body of music included songs such as "This Land Is Your Land" that praised America's people and landscape, demanded the promises of democracy and the benefits of freedom, and cried out in defense of the rights of workers. While most of his work addressed topics of social import, Guthrie, a father of eight—including another iconic folk singer, Arlo Guthrie—revealed childlike qualities in a number of songs inspired by and written for children. While his political leanings were decidedly left, Guthrie served in both the U.S. Merchant Marine and the Army during World War II.

Guthrie lived much of his adult life on the road, tramping across the United States in the years both before and after World War II. His ramblings inspired nomadic elements among the beat and hippie generations that followed—and many emulate his wanderings today. A prolific writer whose body of work includes two autobiographical novels, *Bound for Glory* and *Seeds of Man*, hundreds of songs, thousands of pages of poetry, letters, and other works, has likewise inspired legions of musicians, such as Bob Dylan and Bruce

Springsteen. His work continues to inspire others more than four decades after his death in 1967.

The importance of Guthrie's legacy is reflected in the honors and awards he has received. The year before he died, he was awarded the U.S. Department of the Interior's Conservation Award. Since then, he has received the Folk Alliance Lifetime Achievement Award (1996) and a Lifetime Achievement Award from the National Academy of Recording Arts and Sciences (1999). He has been inducted into the National

FIGURE 1.1 Legendary musician Woody Guthrie died of Huntington's disease at age 55.

Songwriters' Hall of Fame (1971), the Nashville Songwriters' Hall of Fame (1977), the Rock and Roll Hall of Fame and Museum (1988), and the Oklahoma Hall of Fame (2006).

Guthrie's accomplishments are impressive for a man who died at the relatively young age of 55. They are even more impressive considering that he spent most of the final 15 years of his life in hospitals as he slowly succumbed to the ravages of a dreadful disease—Huntington's disease, a progressive genetic disease that slowly destroys nervous system function and control, eventually leading to death.

OKLAHOMA ROOTS

Woodrow Wilson Guthrie was born in Okemah, Oklahoma, on July 14, 1912, to Charley and Nora (Sherman) Guthrie. While his early life seemed relatively normal, tragedy struck in 1919 when his older sister Clara died after setting her clothes on fire following an argument with her equally strong-willed mother. Clara had only intended to scare Nora, putting coal oil on her dress and setting it alight to burn the clothes a bit. She planned to put the flames out quickly, but failed and ran screaming from the house. Neighbors caught up with Clara and smothered the flames with a blanket, but the teenager—severely burned from neck to knees—succumbed soon after. It was not the first bizarre incident in Guthrie's family.

Guthrie's grandfather, George Sherman, died fairly young—drowning in shallow water after falling from a horse. The Shermans had long been plagued by similar tragedies, and with the death of Clara, the dark cloud that had hung over the Sherman family began to pay regular visits to the Guthries' home. The fire that killed Clara was not the first. One family home was destroyed in 1909—only a month after it was built—by a fire started by sparks from a fire in a neighbor's kitchen. Nor was the 1919 fire the last. One night in 1927, Nora set Charley on fire as he napped on a sofa. Like his daughter Clara, Charley fled the house, his clothes in flames. Outside, he fell to the ground and began to roll, and a neighbor helped to extinguish the fire. Charley survived and tried to dismiss the incident as an accident, but others disagreed, and with the consent of Nora's family, he had her committed to Central Oklahoma State Hospital in Norman.

Nora Guthrie had been a proud woman—attractive and attentive to her appearance—but as Woody and his siblings grew up, she began to change. She could be moody and overwhelmed by inexplicable anger at times. She took less interest in and care of her looks. She had bouts of bizarre behavior, such as walking around town sobbing. At home, she would have fits that began with progressive loss of muscle control—first in the face, then the arms and legs—until she could no longer walk. She would roll around on the floor, screaming loudly enough to be heard several blocks away. The family's doctor dismissed it as insanity. Woody's grandmother, Mary (Mahoney) Sherman, suspected a mysterious illness that had plagued the Sherman family.

She was right. While at Central Oklahoma State Hospital, Nora was diagnosed with Huntington's **chorea**—Huntington's disease. Several months later, Woody visited her in a locked ward at the hospital. She sat, her arms and legs jerking uncontrollably. She had lost a lot of weight. She stared into space, not responding to his attempts at conversation. She did not even seem to recognize him. Only as he left did she finally break her silence.

"You're Woody, aren't you?" she asked.[1]

Nora Guthrie died of Huntington's disease in 1929.

NO ESCAPE

As early as 1930, Guthrie knew that the disease was hereditary, but he believed—or tried to convince himself—that he had nothing to worry about. He once told a friend, "There's no way I'm gonna get that disease."[2] Woody married Mary Jennings, the sister of his best friend, Matt, while they lived in Pampa, Texas, in 1933. His restless wanderings across the Depression-era United States took a toll on their marriage. After three children—and a long separation—the pair were finally divorced in 1943.

In the early 1940s, Woody began to suffer bouts of bizarre behavior. Because of his increasing reputation as a troubadour and writer—*Bound for Glory* was published in 1943—the incidents were dismissed as symptoms of excessive alcohol intake, a condition not unfamiliar to many working musicians and writers. While serving in the merchant marine during World War II, however, Guthrie began to suspect something else, once telling a crewmate that he might have the same illness that killed his mother.

After the war, Guthrie's behavior grew more bizarre. Living in New York City with his second wife, Marjorie Greenblatt (whom he married in 1945), he became prone to angry outbursts at home—once coming after her with a knife. In 1948, during a separation from Marjorie, he wrote a series of letters to Mary Crissman, a young woman with whom he was smitten (and the younger sister of Maxine Crissman, one of his former musical partners). The letters, containing a bizarre mixture of love, sex, and violence, aroused concern beyond the Crissman family. (At one point, Los Angeles police considered Guthrie a suspect in the still unsolved murder of Elizabeth Short—the notorious Black Dahlia—in 1947.) While cleared of any suspicion in the Black Dahlia murder, postal officials investigated him for violating the Comstock Law, which prohibited the sending of obscene material in the mail. He pleaded guilty to sending one "obscene, lewd, and lascivious" letter and served a brief term in prison in 1949. Afterward, he could be found wandering aimlessly around New York City, much as his mother had done in his native Oklahoma. He was arrested for loitering and suspected of public drunkenness.

Guthrie's deteriorating condition reached a state of crisis in 1952. By now, his second marriage was all but over. Marjorie had begun seeing someone else, and on the night of May 15, when she returned from a date, she found Guthrie waiting for her in a state bordering on frenzied. He attacked Marjorie with scissors. During the attack, she made a critical observation—he was not drunk at the time. Nonetheless, Marjorie and a group of Guthrie's friends had him checked into Kings County Hospital for alcoholism. The treatment regimen accomplished nothing. The visit to Kings County Hospital was the first in a series of hospitalizations, including one at Bellevue Hospital—the oldest public hospital in the United States and long noted for its pioneering achievements in the diagnosis and treatment of mental diseases—where he was diagnosed with schizophrenia. Again, the treatments accomplished nothing. After his release from Bellevue, Guthrie paid Marjorie and their three surviving children (including Arlo; their first child, Cathy, died in an electrical fire at their home in 1947) a visit on Arlo's birthday. The visit ended when Guthrie became angry and hit Marjorie and some of the children. Guthrie checked himself back into Bellevue. The doctors there were stumped.

Guthrie checked into Brooklyn State Hospital on July 22 in the hope that its experimental treatments with alcoholism might help. Marjorie, who accompanied him, suspected more than alcoholism and pleaded with the doctors there to find another cause. For nearly six weeks, little progress was made—despite the fact that one physician noted that Guthrie's condition incorporated "elements of schizophrenia, psychopathy and a psychoneurotic anxiety state, not to mention the personality changes occurring in Huntington's chorea."[3] The dithering diagnoses continued until September 3, when a young doctor noticed Guthrie's mother had also been hospitalized in a mental institution with an undiagnosed illness and asked, "How come no one has said this guy has Huntington's chorea?"[4] The diagnosis stuck, but nearly three weeks passed before the physicians shared the news with Guthrie.

Guthrie left the hospital on September 24, and on Marjorie's suggestion, took off with another musician, Ramblin' Jack Elliott, for a trip across the country. In California, he met and began a relationship with another woman, Anneke van Kirk. In 1953, he divorced Marjorie and married Anneke in time for the birth of their daughter. But the progressing disease took its toll. After a sojourn in Florida, Guthrie returned to New York and checked himself back into Brooklyn State Hospital on September 16, 1954. His third marriage fell apart as Anneke could not cope with the burden of caring for him. She filed for divorce soon after his return to the hospital. Marjorie, who had remarried, stepped up to help take care of Guthrie after that.

Toward the end of the 1950s, Guthrie's reputation as an icon of American music grew. The folk music scene that helped lay the foundation of rock and roll acknowledged Guthrie as one of its pioneers—in fact, many of the leaders of that movement, such as Ramblin' Jack Elliott and Pete Seeger, had played with Guthrie on a number of occasions. A young Robert Zimmerman, later known as Bob Dylan, visited Guthrie in his later years.

Despite the accolades, Guthrie's health deteriorated. Because of increasing loss of muscle control, Guthrie spent

FIGURE 1.2 Woody Guthrie (*left, with cigarette*), deeply afflicted with Huntington's disease, receives the U.S. Department of Interior Conservation Service Award in 1966. His former wife Marjorie Guthrie and his son Arlo look on.

his final years in a series of hospitals before Huntington's disease ended his life on October 3, 1967, at Creedmoor State Hospital in Queens, New York.

The deadly legacy that stalked Guthrie's family continued to plague his children. Three—Bill, with Mary; Cathy, with Marjorie; and Lorina Lynn, with Anneke—died prematurely in accidents. Two, Gwendolyn and Sue (both with Mary) died of Huntington's disease. Only the surviving children with Marjorie—Arlo (born 1947), Joady Ben (born 1948), and Nora (born 1950)—seem to have escaped the legacy of the disease that claimed their grandmother, father, and two half sisters.

2

DANCE AND DISCOVERY

When Woody Guthrie was diagnosed with Huntington's disease, among the symptoms listed was **St. Vitus's dance**. Huntington's disease has long been linked to the appearance of dancing. The word *chorea*—the second part of the original name for Huntington's disease—is based upon a Greek term for a dance. As the disease progresses, brain cells die and patients lose control of their muscles. Arms flail, the body rocks back and forth, the feet shuffle, and the mouth hardens into a grimace—all movements that mimic normal, voluntary actions, but that instead occur at random, sometimes wildly, without coordination or individual control. The person's behavior may likewise be affected, with typically mild, stable individuals erupting into violent outbursts or engaging in other unusual acts. The frenetic activity resembles that of manic dancers of times past.

Reports of wild, uncontrollable, violent dances accumulated for thousands of years. Some of the earliest reports concerned the Phrygians—an ancient people who lived in Anatolia (now Turkey)—who, in their worship of the goddess Cybele, drank, drummed, and danced themselves into a state of ecstasy. While lost in their religious frenzy, worshippers often mutilated themselves—men even ritually castrated themselves to join the goddess's priestly class of the *gallae*. Such bizarre behavior during their frenzied dances became a hallmark of dancing manias and of later conditions such as Huntington's chorea.

THE DANCE OF DEATH

Whether the inspiration came from whirling dervishes or pre-Christian pagan traditions, outbreaks of mass frenzied dancing spread through Europe during the Middle Ages. Among the best known was the **dance of St. John**, so wild, uncontrollable, and violent that Roman Catholic authorities believed practitioners were

Medieval depiction of the dance of death, later known as the dance of St. John or St. Vitus's dance

possessed by the devil. The phenomenon grew in prominence as millions of Europeans were dying during the Black Plague. In *The Epidemics of the Middle Ages*, J.F.C. Hecker states:

> The effects of the *Black Death* had not yet subsided, and the graves of millions of its victims were scarcely closed, when a strange delusion arose in Germany, which took possession of the minds of men, and, in spite of the divinity of our nature, hurried away body and soul into the magic circle of hellish superstition. It was a convulsion which in the most extraordinary manner infuriated the human frame, and excited the astonishment of contemporaries for more

Even as the Phrygian religion died out, similar dance traditions carried on. Shortly after the founding of Islam, one sect, the Sufi, whose members are sometimes called dervishes, began practicing a whirling meditative dance

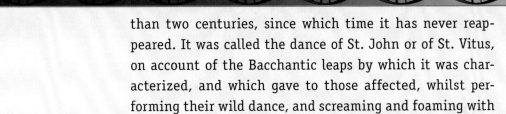

than two centuries, since which time it has never reappeared. It was called the dance of St. John or of St. Vitus, on account of the Bacchantic leaps by which it was characterized, and which gave to those affected, whilst performing their wild dance, and screaming and foaming with fury, all the appearance of persons possessed. It did not remain confined to particular localities, but was propagated by the sight of the sufferers, like a demoniacal epidemic, over the whole of Germany and the neighbouring countries to the north-west, which were already prepared for its reception by the prevailing opinions of the times.[5]

An observer described such a scene that took place in Aix-la-Chappelle (modern Aachen, Germany) in 1374. The dancers gathered in circles, hand in hand, and moved in a delirious frenzy. Some saw spirits and called out their names. Others saw Jesus Christ and the Virgin Mary. They danced until they collapsed from exhaustion, recovered, and danced again. Some eventually collapsed from epilepsy-like convulsions, foaming at the mouth and struggling for breath. The mania known as the dance of St. John spread through Germany, the Low Countries, and into France. Peasants and tradesmen abandoned their lives to join in the revelry. Priests in cities like Liege, certain that the problem was triggered by devilish forces, battled the phenomenon with exorcisms and other spiritual treatments.

characterized by wild, uncontrollable movements. The dance was often accompanied by spasms and convulsions, even ritual mutilation—though the acts of mutilation were not as extreme as those of men aspiring to join Cybele's priestly class. At the time of his death, Sir Richard Francis Burton, a nineteenth-century English explorer believed to have converted to the Sufi sect of Islam, was found with many knife or sword scars on his body that were best explained by participation in such Sufi ceremonies.

Europeans, who as far back as the Phrygians had crazed dance traditions of their own, may have been exposed to dervish practices during the latter Crusades—a series of religiously motivated military campaigns launched by Christian Europe during the years 1095 to 1302 in an effort to take Jerusalem and the Holy Land from its Muslim rulers. Christians in Muslim Europe, such as Spain, Portugal, and the Balkans, would likewise have been exposed to the dervishes.

ST. VITUS'S DANCE

St. Vitus's dance first appeared in Strasbourg in 1418. The symptoms in many ways paralleled that of the dance of St. John. A group of people would start dancing uncontrollably through the streets. Spectators would join the group, first as followers, and later as fellow participants. The manic throng might dance for days, forgoing food, only stopping when they were either cured of the dancing mania or dead. Instead of exorcism, Good Samaritans began taking the afflicted to chapels devoted to St. Vitus, the patron saint of actors, comedians, and dancers (and epileptics). There they prayed to the saint, martyred during the reign of Roman emperor Diocletian (284–305), for help. In time, St. Vitus also became the patron saint of those affected by the dance that eventually bore his name.

FIGURE 2.2   Pieter Brueghel's *Pilgrimage of the Epileptics to the Church at Molenbeek*

While the movement and behavioral anomalies associated with chorea continued to be linked with spiritual disorders as late as the seventeenth century—some researchers suspect some of the victims of the Salem witch trials may have suffered from Huntington's disease because of the bizarre and at times uncontrollable actions that aroused the suspicions of their accusers—modern science began seeking natural explanations for the phenomena. Paracelsus (1493–1541), the famous sixteenth-century alchemist, astrologer, and physician, helped transform medicine into the scientifically based discipline it is now. He enjoyed tweaking the noses of the establishment, openly and sarcastically criticizing the prevailing (but outmoded) wisdom. He explained his views about seeking natural causes for disease in characteristically blunt fashion: "We will not however admit that the saints have power to inflict diseases, and that these ought to be named after them, although many there are, who in their theology lay great stress on this supposition, ascribing them rather to God than to nature, which is but idle talk. We dislike such nonsensical gossip as is not supported by symptoms, but only by faith, a thing which is not human, whereon the gods themselves set no value."[6]

Paracelsus took an interest in dancing mania and related disorders, and he coined the term *chorea* to describe the rapid, jerky motions characteristic of people in the throes of mania or of something of more organic origin. He classified chorea disorders into three types: chorea *imaginativa*, or chorea triggered by imagination; chorea *lascivus*, or chorea triggered by sensual desires; and chorea *naturalis*, or chorea triggered by physical causes such as illness. In Paracelsus's description of someone afflicted with chorea naturalis, one can discern elements of modern, rather than medieval, disorders recognized as chorea.

THOMAS SYDENHAM AND CHOREA

A century after Paracelsus's work, Thomas Sydenham (1624–1689) clarified some of the understanding of chorea, but confused it as well. In his description of *chorus Sancti Viti*, or St. Vitus's dance, he gave a fairly clear definition of the symptoms of chorea.

> There is a kind of convulsion, which attacks boys and girls from the tenth year to the time of puberty. It first shows itself by limping or unsteadiness in one of the legs, which the patient drags. The hand cannot be steady for a moment. It passes from one position to another by a convulsive

movement, however much the patient may strive to the contrary. Before he can raise a cup to his lips, he does make as many gesticulations as a mountebank; since he does not move it in a straight line, but has his hand drawn aside by the spasms, until by some good fortune he brings it at last to his mouth. He then gulps it off at once, so suddenly and so greedily as to look as if he were trying to amuse the lookers-on.[7]

In using the term *St. Vitus's dance*, however, Sydenham confused mass dance mania—of whatever cause—with a disease of purely physical origin that affects individuals rather than groups. He also failed to mention the association of the chorea he described with **rheumatic fever**, the result of a bacterial infection. That connection was firmly established by Richard Bright (1797–1858). Unlike the disease that claimed the life of Woody Guthrie, this predominantly childhood chorea resolved itself—diminished—over time. Although still referred to as St. Vitus's dance, today the movement disorder described by Sydenham is more often referred to as Sydenham's chorea.

By the nineteenth century, others were noticing that another form of St. Vitus's dance primarily affected adults. John Elliotson (1791–1868) in particular described the effects of the adult-onset disease.

When it occurs in adults, it is frequently connected with paralysis or idiotism, and will perhaps never be cured. It is very rare for you to remove the affection if it occurs in an adult, or if it occurs in a local form. It will sometimes take place in one arm, or in the head, or in some of the muscles of the face, so that the person makes faces continually. In cases of this description I have never seen the affection cured. It then appears to arise for the most part from

FIGURE 2.3   Thomas Sydenham was a pioneer in the scientific study of choreas.

something in the original constitution of the body, for I have often seen it hereditary.[8]

Elliotson's description is significant because he mentions that the disease is often hereditary—it can be passed from parent to child—but there are problems with the passage as well. Elliotson, like Sydenham, confused Sydenham's chorea with Huntington's disease in that he did not differentiate the curable childhood disorder from the fatal, incurable disease that usually appears later in life.

Nevertheless, several physicians, all working in the middle of the nineteenth century, independently described a hereditary, chronic, typically adult-onset form of St. Vitus's dance that would eventually be named Huntington's disease.

THE MAGRUMS

The first to clearly describe a hereditary, chronic, adult-onset disease was the Reverend Charles Oscar Waters (1816–1892), also a trained physician, who lived in upstate New York. He described the symptoms and prognosis of a hereditary chorea that descendants of Dutch settlers in the region called the "magrums." In an 1841 letter to Robley Dunglison, his former professor, Waters wrote:

> It consists essentially of a spasmodic action of all, or nearly all, the voluntary muscles of the system, of involuntary and more or less irregular motions of the extremities, face and trunk. . . . The expression of the countenance and general appearance of the patient are very much as are described as characteristic of chorea. . . .
>
> This singular disease rarely, very rarely indeed, makes its appearance before adult life, and attacks after forty-five

years of age are also very rare. When once it has appeared, however, it clings to its suffering victim with unrelenting tenacity until death comes to his relief. It very rarely or never ceases while life lasts.

The first indications of its appearance are spasmodic twitching of the extremities, generally of the fingers, which gradually extend and involve all of the voluntary muscles. This derangement of muscular action is by no means uniform; in some cases it exists to a greater, in others to a less extent, but in all cases it gradually induces a state of more or less perfect dementia.

When speaking of the manifestly hereditary nature of the disease, I should perhaps have remarked that I have never known a case of it to occur in a patient, one or both of whose ancestors were not, with the third generation at farthest, the subject of this distressing malady.[9]

In 1848, not long after Waters described hereditary chorea in his letter to Dunglison, Charles Rollins Gorman (1817–1879) is said to have described a similar disease in a dissertation at Jefferson Medical College in Philadelphia. Several contemporaries referred to the work; unfortunately, the original work has since been lost and no copies have ever been found.

Irving Whitehall Lyon (1840–1896) was a physician who grew up in the town of Bedford, Westchester County, New York. He earned medical degrees from the University of Vermont (1862) and the College of Physicians and Surgeons at Columbia University in New York City (1863). From 1863 to 1864 he served on the staff of Bellevue Hospital in New York City. He published his study of hereditary chorea in 1863, focusing on several families in Westchester and adjacent portions of Connecticut who, like the families described by

Waters, displayed symptoms of a hereditary, adult-onset chorea. Lyon mentioned similar local names for the disease as Waters did—some variant of "magrums" or "migrims"— which has led some scholars to conclude both men may have used some of the same families as subjects in their respective accounts. (Waters's letter was vague on location, other than being from somewhere in the southeastern portion of New York.) Lyon wrote:

> The writer has been familiar from childhood with a type of chorea so unlike in its *origin* to anything described in our standard textbooks, that the publication of a few facts in relation thereto has been thought advisable, not only as a matter of interest to the reader, but more especially for the purpose of eliciting the observations of any who may have met with indications of kindred significance.
>
> The peculiarity of origin claimed for this type consists in its hereditary transmissibility. . . . It is confined almost exclusively to certain families, so that such are popularly denominated the "migrim families;" and the children of parents affected with this disorder are very liable to become the subjects of its manifestations, and in turn transmit it to their offspring.[10]

Similar observations on the connections between heredity and a debilitating, adult-onset chorea were being made elsewhere. Johan Christian Lund (1830–1906), a district physician in Saetersdal, Norway, offered detailed descriptions of the disease in the *Report of Health and Medical Conditions in Norway* in 1860 and 1868. The descriptions were complete with pedigrees and details of two Saetersdal family groups, the Byglands and Valle families, afflicted by the disease. Because of the rather obscure nature of the publications—government documents—Lund's work went largely unnoticed until it was rediscovered in 1914. Lund referred to the disease as chorea St. Vitus.

> As recorded in the previous medical report, chorea St. Vitus seems to recur as a hereditary disease in Saetersdal. It is commonly known as the "twitches," occasionally as the "inherited disease." It usually occurs between the ages of 50 and 60, generally starting with less obvious symptoms, which at times only progress slowly, without becoming violent, so that the patient's normal activities are not particularly hindered; but more often after a few years they increase to a considerable degree, so that any form of work becomes impossible and even eating becomes difficult and circuitous. The entire body, though chiefly the head, arms, and trunk, is in constant jerking and flinging motion, except during sleep, when the patient is usually motionless. A couple of the severely affected patients have during the last days of their lives become [demented].[11]

The work of Gorman, Lyon, Lund, and Waters all contained accurate descriptions of a hereditary, adult-onset form of chorea that as yet had no name for itself—the name *St. Vitus's dance* was shared with at least one other disorder, Sydenham's chorea. Their work had little influence on the medical community. The individual most responsible for giving the disease a separate identity, whose work had a lasting effect on medical science, was a Long Islander with a family history of practicing medicine. His name was George Huntington.

3

GEORGE HUNTINGTON AND HUNTINGTON'S DISEASE

George Huntington (1850–1916) was born and raised in East Hampton, then a small town in eastern Long Island, New York. As a young man, he took up the family business—medicine. His grandfather, Abel Huntington (1777–1858), moved to East Hampton from Connecticut in 1797, shortly after completing his medical studies at the Connecticut Medical Convention. George Huntington's father, George Lee Huntington (1811–1881), earned his medical degree from New York University and Medical School and carried on the family practice in East Hampton.

As a boy, George Huntington accompanied his father on his rounds, so it is no surprise that he, too, was inspired to pursue medicine as a career. He conducted his medical studies at the College of Physicians and Surgeons at Columbia University in New York City, graduating in 1871. After working briefly with his father in East Hampton, he moved west to Pomeroy, Ohio, to begin his own practice. He had not been a professional physician long before he read his paper, "On Chorea," at a meeting of the Meigs and Mason Academy of Medicine in Middleport, Ohio, on February 15, 1872. The paper was published in the *Medical and Surgical Reporter: A Weekly Journal* on April 13, 1872.

FIGURE 3.1   Huntington's disease was named after George Huntington, whose work on the study of chorea led to scholars around the world taking note of this disease.

Huntington, in a brief memoir published in 1910, wrote that both his grandfather and father had long been aware of the disease, having treated members of families afflicted by it. He described his first experience with the disease: "Driving with my father through a wooded road leading from Easthampton to Amagansett, we suddenly came upon two women, mother and daughter, both bowing, twisting, grimacing. I stared in wonderment, almost in fear. What could it mean?"[12]

Huntington began researching the disease in earnest while working with his father in East Hampton. His father edited his manuscript for "On Chorea" before George moved to Ohio to begin his own practice. Much of the paper was a general discussion of chorea—particularly of Sydenham's chorea. The discussion of hereditary chorea closed the manuscript:

> And now I wish to draw your attention more particularly to a form of the disease which exists, so far as I know, almost exclusively on the east end of Long Island. It is peculiar in itself and seems to obey certain fixed laws. In the first place, let me remark that chorea, as it is commonly known to the profession, and a description of which I have already given, is of exceedingly rare occurrence there. I do not remember a single instance occurring in my father's practice, and I have often heard him say that it was a rare disease and seldom met with by him.
>
> The hereditary chorea, as I shall call it, is confined to certain and fortunately a few families, and has been transmitted to them, an heirloom from generations away back in the dim past. It is spoken of by those in whose veins the seeds of the disease are known to exist, with a kind of horror, and not at all alluded to except through dire necessity, when it is mentioned as "that disorder." It is attended

generally by all the symptoms of common chorea, only in an aggravated degree, hardly ever manifesting itself until adult or middle life, and then coming on gradually but surely, increasing by degrees, and often occupying years in its development, until the hapless sufferer is but a quivering wreck of his former self.

It is as common and is indeed, I believe, more common among men than women, while I am not aware that season or complexion has any influence in the matter. There are three marked peculiarities in this disease: 1. Its hereditary nature. 2. A tendency to insanity and suicide. 3. Its manifesting itself as a grave disease only in adult life.

1. Of its hereditary nature. When either or both the parents have shown manifestations of the disease, and more especially when these manifestations have been of a serious nature, one or more of the offspring almost invariably suffer from the disease, if they live to adult age. But if by any chance these children go through life without it, the thread is broken and the grandchildren and great-grandchildren of the original shakers may rest assured that they are free from the disease. This you will perceive differs from the general laws of so-called hereditary diseases, as for instance in phthisis, or syphilis, when one generation may enjoy entire immunity from their dread ravages, and yet in another you find them cropping out in all their hideousness. Unstable and whimsical as the disease may be in other respects, in this it is firm, it never skips a generation to again manifest itself in another; once having yielded its claims, it never regains them. In all the families, or nearly all in which the choreic [chorea-like] taint exists, the nervous temperament greatly preponderates, and in my grandfather's and father's experience, which

conjointly cover a period of 78 years, nervous excitement in a marked degree almost invariably attends upon every disease these people may suffer from, although they may not when in health be over nervous.

2. The tendency to insanity, and sometimes that form of insanity which leads to suicide, is marked. I know of several instances of suicide of people suffering from this form of chorea, or who belonged to families in which the disease existed. As the disease progresses the mind becomes more or less impaired, in many amounting to insanity, while in others mind and body both gradually fail until death relieves them of their sufferings. At present I know of two married men, whose wives are living, and who are constantly making love to some young lady, not seeming to be aware that there is any impropriety in it. They are suffering from chorea to such an extent that they can hardly walk, and would be thought, by a stranger, to be intoxicated. They are men of about 50 years of age, but never let an opportunity to flirt with a girl go past unimproved. The effect is ridiculous in the extreme.

3. Its third peculiarity is its coming on, at least as a grave disease, only in adult life. I do not know of a single case that has shown any marked signs of chorea before the age of thirty or forty years, while those who pass the fortieth year without symptoms of the disease, are seldom attacked. It begins as an ordinary chorea might begin, by the irregular and spasmodic action of certain muscles, as of the face, arms, etc. These movements gradually increase, when muscles hitherto unaffected take on the spasmodic action, until every muscle in the body becomes affected (excepting the involuntary ones), and the poor patient presents a spectacle which is anything but pleasing to witness. I have never known

a recovery or even an amelioration of symptoms in this form of chorea; when once it begins it clings to the bitter end. No treatment seems to be of any avail, and indeed nowadays its end is so well-known to the sufferer and his friends, that medical advice is seldom sought. It seems at least to be one of the incurables.[13]

Huntington closed his paper with the suggestion that his colleagues "may have some interest" in the phenomenon. He was correct. Scholars around the world took note of the disease and began to study it in detail. Within two decades, other researchers, such as William Osler in his book *On Chorea and Choreiform Affections*, had begun referring to the disease as Huntington's chorea. By 1908, more than 200 publications on the disease had followed Huntington's 1872 paper.

Osler gave Huntington's work high praise when he wrote, "In the history of medicine there are few instances in which a disease has been more accurately, more graphically, or more briefly described."[14]

THE DISEASE

Huntington's chorea is better known today as Huntington's disease—a genetic **neurodegenerative disease** that erodes an affected person's control over movement and behavior. It leads to death.

The disease typically appears near the time of a person's fortieth birthday, although it can appear much earlier. The first symptoms of the disease are often behavioral changes—unusual mood swings and increased irritability. The person may seem more aggressive and angry; conversely, he or she may seem more passive and depressed. Compulsions may become exaggerated. An affected person may be more likely to abuse alcohol or drugs, gamble recklessly, or engage in

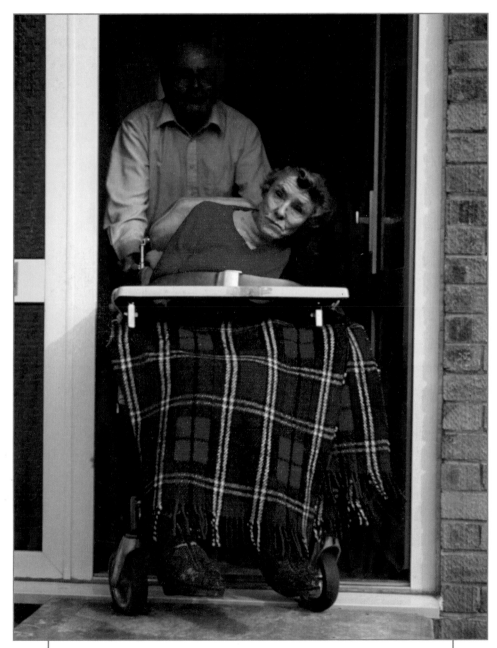

FIGURE 3.2   The physical symptoms of uncontrolled movement often lead to wheelchair confinement in patients in advanced stages of Huntington's disease.

sexual excess. In time, the behavioral disturbances often diminish, but as they do, other symptoms worsen.

Among the worsening symptoms are **cognitive** changes. The person with Huntington's disease may have more trouble thinking, planning, or solving problems. Memory—long-term, short-term, as well as of how to accomplish routine tasks—may be impaired. Muscle control is adversely affected, as is sensory perception, the ability to properly process and assign meaning to sensory stimuli, and spatial perception, the ability to know where one's body, or parts of it, are located with respect to other objects. For example, as spatial perception is diminished, people in the early stages of Huntington's disease may be bruised from repeatedly running into furniture and the like.

Disturbances in sensory perception may range from mild events—like sensing movement in the periphery of one's vision—to hallucinations (perceptions without stimuli). As his condition worsened, Woody Guthrie reported hearing voices and seeing people, such as Jesus Christ, talking to him. One change that may have drastic effects on personal relationships is loss of the ability to initiate appropriate behaviors—such as maintaining personal hygiene—and to inhibit inappropriate ones. The letter writing that got Woody Guthrie in trouble was an example of inability to inhibit inappropriate behavior, as were his sudden eruptions into violence.

The most devastating effects, however, are the physical ones. The term *chorea*—a Greek word for a type of dance—was used to describe the uncontrollable, jerky movements that characterize the disease. The onset may be subtle, such as a person spilling more coffee from their morning cup than usual. The person may bump into others and bang into furniture, causing them to wonder why the sudden clumsiness. In

OTHER CHOREAS

Sydenham's chorea: Sydenham's chorea, also known today as St. Vitus's dance, is an inflammatory complication of rheumatic fever. The fever is caused by infection by Streptococcus bacteria. Sydenham's chorea, which occurs in about 20% of rheumatic fever patients (usually children and teens), is characterized by rapid, random, involuntary movements. Choreic symptoms usually end within a few months.

Chorea gravidarum: Chorea gravidarum occurs during pregnancy, usually in women with a history of rheumatic fever. It usually ends after labor.

Hemiballismus: Hemiballismus is a violent flinging of arms or legs on one side of the body. Generally it is caused by tumors, seizures, or damage to parts of the basal ganglia—a part of the brain involved in regulating movement. It usually ends within a few weeks after it appears.

Drug-induced choreas: A number of drugs, such as levodopa (used for the treatment of Parkinson's disease), anticonvulsants, and antipsychotics, may have choreic side effects. Symptoms can be controlled by adjusting dosages.

Metabolic, endocrine, and other conditions that cause chorea: Symptoms and treatment depend on the specific cause. Metabolic choreas can be caused by liver disease, alcohol abuse, or hypoglycemia. Hypothyroidism and other endocrine disorders, which affect hormone levels, may likewise trigger choreic symptoms. Symptoms of chorea may be triggered by other conditions that damage or affect brain cells, such as strokes.

time, movements become more exaggerated, with the arms flailing and the body contorting randomly as if the person is drunk. Muscles of the face are affected as well, with the person unable to prevent him- or herself from grimacing or making bizarre faces. The person may slur his or her speech, reinforcing the impression of intoxication.

As the disease progresses, any function that requires muscle control is affected. The person loses the ability to chew or swallow. Many Huntington's patients lose weight as a result of their inability to get adequate nutrition. Sleep, too, may be disturbed—even rapid eye movements characteristic of the dream state may be disrupted. In time, dementia sets in.

The combination of physical, mental, and emotional effects renders people with Huntington's disease incapable of taking care of themselves. Most persons with Huntington's disease die within 10 to 30 years of the onset of symptoms.

In a small percentage of cases, symptoms of Huntington's disease can appear in a person before the age of 21. Such early onset is referred to as juvenile Huntington's disease. Instead of rapid, uncontrollable, jerky movement characteristic of chorea, juvenile Huntington's disease may be accompanied by stiffness or rigidness. Recurrent seizures are common as well. Disease progression and death occur more rapidly in the juvenile form of the disease, usually within 10 years of the first appearance of symptoms.

THE NUMBERS

According to the U.S. National Institute of Neurological Disorders and Stroke, about 15,000 Americans have Huntington's disease, for a **prevalence** of about 5 cases per 100,000 individuals. Less than 10% of those cases occur in juveniles.

Another 150,000 Americans have at least a 50% risk of inheriting the disease. Globally, the prevalence ranges from less than 1 per 100,000 to as high as 17 per 100,000. While the disease is reported worldwide, it is highest in populations of European descent or with some European ancestry. The lowest prevalence rates are in Asia, with data from one region of Japan as low as 0.1 per 100,000. The juvenile form of the disease makes up about 5% of Huntington's cases worldwide.

One study from China found that Huntington's disease prevalence is highest near the coast—in particular, near port cities frequented by Europeans over the last few centuries. In Africa, patterns are similar, with prevalence rates higher in populations with a greater degree of European ancestry. The disease is virtually absent in Native Americans and Aboriginal Australians. These and other data all suggest that the disease originated in European populations and spread as Europeans dispersed around the globe, especially in the past 500 years.

THE MONK AND
THE SKEPTIC

At the time George Huntington presented his paper, "On Chorea," very little was understood about the nature of heredity. Without that understanding, discovering the cause of the disease—and ultimately the treatment or a cure—would be next to impossible.

Humans had long understood that offspring tended to inherit characteristics of their parents—this had been the basis of selective breeding of plants and animals, a practice that had existed for several thousand years. Charles Darwin (1809–1882) and Alfred Russel Wallace (1823–1913) likewise used that awareness in independently developing a theory of evolution by natural selection. Neither man understood how characteristics of parents were passed down to offspring, however, nor were they familiar with the work of the monk Gregor Mendel (1822–1884), whose agricultural experiments at the Augustinian Abbey of St. Thomas in Brno (in what is now the Czech Republic) revealed the basic principles of inheritance. In fact, few had taken notice of Mendel's work, originally presented in 1865 and published in 1866, until the turn of the twentieth century. Darwin himself appears to have been unaware of Mendel's research. If he had read Mendel's paper, it may have helped him avoid some mistaken ideas he embraced

38

FIGURE 4.1 Because of Gregor Mendel, we now understand how diseases like Huntington's disease can be inherited through generations.

about how novel characteristics arose and were passed down to later generations.

MENDEL'S QUESTION

Mendel began his research with a basic question. Was a particular characteristic in offspring the result of a blend of heritable—that is, being passed on from parent to child—factors from each parent? Or were the heritable factors passed down in discrete particulate units that retained their identity in the offspring and were likewise passed down intact to subsequent generations?

To better understand the problem, consider a hypothetical color **gene** (what Mendel referred to as a heritable factor) with two initial variants, red and blue. According to the blending hypothesis, if a red parent passed down the red variant and a blue parent passed down a blue variant, the color of the offspring would be purple. The copies of the gene inside the offspring would likewise be purple. When the offspring became a parent, instead of passing down a red or blue variant of the gene, it would pass down the newly blended purple variant.

If Mendel's heritable factors where passed in discrete units—that is, the particulate hypothesis—then the offspring of a red parent and a blue one might likewise still be purple, but each copy of the gene it carried, and ultimately passed down to its offspring, would still retain the original red or blue identity.

Students typically learn that Mendel tackled the problem by working with pea (*Pisum sativum*) plants. In fact, he worked with several plant species, but peas gave the clearest results. Peas had a number of characteristics that made them suitable for Mendel's research: (1) they had many varieties, therefore many different characteristics to work with; (2) they were true breeders, so that a plant of one variety would give rise to offspring of the same variety; and (3) they were self-pollinating, enabling him to devise controlled crossbreeding experiments among different varieties. Mendel would snip the pollen-producing (male) flower parts from some plants—so they could not pollinate themselves—then take pollen from a different variety and dust it on the seed-producing (female) flower parts of the plants that had had the male parts snipped off. He recorded the characteristics of the parent plants (the P generation), then recorded the characteristics of the offspring. Mendel then crossbred the first-generation (F1) offspring in the same way he had done the initial cross. He noted the characteristics of the second-generation (F2) offspring. In many cases, he repeated the crossing experiments for several generations.

Mendel, as a result of his work, rejected the blending hypothesis of inheritance in favor of the particulate hypothesis. Not only that, he made a number of other findings that give him undisputed recognition as the "Father of Genetics." First, characteristics that vary within a population often vary because there are alternate versions (**alleles**) of the heritable factor (gene) that produces the characteristic. Second, organisms in sexually reproducing organisms typically carry two alleles for each gene—they receive one allele from each parent.

Mendel found that for some traits one allele is **dominant** over others. Consider the red/blue example, except that in this case, the red allele is dominant over the blue one. The blue allele in this case would be called **recessive**. If an individual inherits two red alleles (**homozygous** dominant), or a red allele and a blue one (**heterozygous**), it will be red. The only way an individual could be blue is if it inherited two copies of the blue allele (homozygous recessive).

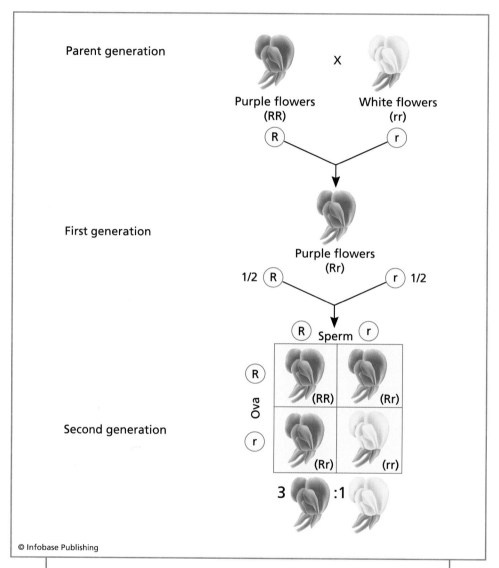

Parent generation

Purple flowers
(RR)

X

White flowers
(rr)

R

r

First generation

Purple flowers
(Rr)

1/2 R

r 1/2

R   Sperm   r

Ova

R

(RR)

(Rr)

Second generation

r

(Rr)

(rr)

3   :1

© Infobase Publishing

FIGURE 4.2   Mendel's experiment involved breeding generations of pea plants to see how the flowers' color was inherited from generation to generation.

For other traits, however, if an individual inherits two different alleles, the resulting characteristic is a blend of that coded for by each allele, such as in the previous example where a cross between an individual with a red allele (variant) and one with a blue allele produces an offspring that is purple. This is known as **incomplete dominance**. Even though the resulting trait is a blend of the two parental characteristics, the heritable units retain their identity in keeping with the particulate hypothesis. This could be confirmed by crossing purple parents. Their offspring should be a mixture of red individuals, blue individuals, and purple individuals.

Mendel derived two laws of inheritance from his findings. The first is the law of segregation. As stated before, sexually reproducing organisms typically carry two alleles for each gene. According to Mendel's law of segregation, the two alleles separate (segregate) so that an egg cell or sperm cell produced by an individual only carries one of the alleles.

The second law that Mendel derived is the law of independent assortment. It addresses the inheritance of several characteristics at once. According to the law of independent assortment, alleles of one gene segregate independently of alleles of other genes. As a result, descendants of individuals with contrasting traits can develop combinations of characteristics never before seen in their ancestors.

To better understand the law of independent assortment, consider again the red/blue example—keeping in mind that the red allele is dominant—and add another characteristic, say height, that is likewise controlled by a single gene. There are two values for height, tall (recessive) versus short (dominant). First, cross a red, short individual (assume it is homozygous dominant in both cases) with a blue, tall individual (homozygous recessive in both cases). The F1 generation will all be red and short, but they are all heterozygous, with a red and a blue allele for color and a short and a tall allele for height. Second, cross two F1 individuals. The F2 generation will have four possible combinations of characteristics: red and short, red and tall, blue and short, and blue and tall. The red/tall and blue/short combinations did not exist in either the parental generation or the F1 generation—this is independent assortment.

Mendel's genetics research all but ended in 1868 when he was elevated to abbot and administrative duties consumed his time. For the next 30 years, his paper attracted little attention—either other researchers were unaware of it, or those who were aware of it failed to understand the paper or its implications. That changed around 1900 when Hugo de Vries (1848–1935), Carl Correns (1864–1933), and Erich von Tschermak (1871–1962) independently rediscovered Mendel's paper and replicated the results. A Cambridge researcher, William Bateson (1861–1926), became a devotee of Mendel after reading de Vries's and Correns's papers on Mendelian inheritance and realizing their significance. Bateson became the leading evangelist of Mendel's word in the English-speaking world. His book, *Mendel's Principles of Heredity: A Defence* (1902), offered the first English-language translations of Mendel's two research papers on the topic, rebutted Mendel's critics, and elaborated on his ideas.

Chromosomes are structures that become visible in the nucleus of cells when they divide to form two identical clones of the parent cell via a process called **mitosis**. Mitosis occurs during asexual reproduction of single-celled organisms, as well as during growth, development, and renewal of tissues in multicellular organisms. Chromosomes also become visible during the formation of **germ cells** via a process called **meiosis**. All **somatic cells** (non-germ cells) have two copies of each chromosome (with the exception of **sex chromosomes** in genetically normal human males, which have two different types of chromosomes—an X chromosome and a Y chromosome). Special cells that form germ cells, but have yet to begin meiosis, likewise

THE CARRIER OF INFORMATION

Mendel's work, even as it was being celebrated in scientific circles, raised other questions of importance, such as where are the genes located? August Weismann (1834–1914) suggested that the material that carried genes was located in the nucleus of cells. He likewise suggested that it was carried on a molecule that could be divided among the germ cells (egg or sperm cells), so that when an egg and sperm cell fused together to form a zygote, the zygote had a full complement of information required to develop into a new, fully functioning individual. He proposed that genes were carried on a structure he called the "id." Weismann wrote:

> The formation of hybrids proves that the two parents together transmit all their specific characters, so that in the process of fertilization each contributes a hereditary substance which contains the primary constituents of all parts of the organism—that is, all the determinants required for building up a new individual. The hereditary substance becomes halved at the final stage of development of the germ-cells, and consequently all the determinants must previously have been grouped into at least two ids. . . .
>
> It cannot be stated with certainty which portions of the elements of the germ-plasm observable in the nucleus of the ovum correspond to ids, though it is probable that only parts of, and not the entire "chromosomes," are to be regarded as such.[15]

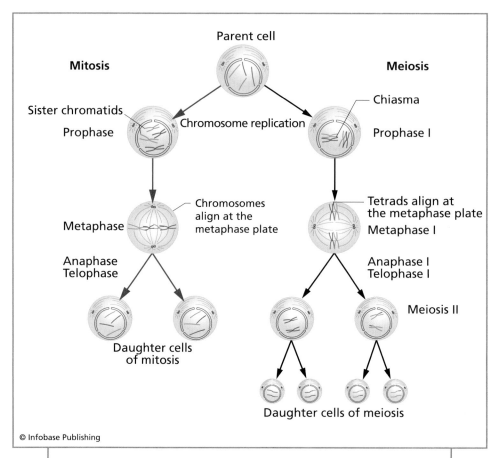

Mitosis

Meiosis

Parent cell

Sister chromatids

Prophase

Chromosome replication

Chiasma

Prophase I

Metaphase

Chromosomes align at the metaphase plate

Tetrads align at the metaphase plate

Metaphase I

Anaphase
Telophase

Anaphase I
Telophase I

Meiosis II

Daughter cells of mitosis

Daughter cells of meiosis

© Infobase Publishing

FIGURE 4.3 In mitosis, which happens in autosomal (or non-sex) cells, a parent cell produces two daughter cells that are genetically the same as the parent. In meiosis, which happens with sex cells, four daughter cells are produced from a precursor cell that has two copies of each chromosome. The four daughter cells contain only one copy of each chromosome.

have two copies of each chromosome. During meiosis, as Weismann predicted, the cells that give rise to germ cells undergo two divisions that produce four cells that have only one copy of each chromosome (and only one sex chromosome).

Weismann's guess that genes were carried on parts of the chromosomes proved to be pretty good, although it would take the work of others, in particular Thomas Hunt Morgan, to amass the evidence to prove it.

THE SKEPTIC

Despite the growing evidence that chromosomes were involved in the transmission of genetic material, many were skeptical of the chromosomal theory of inheritance. Among them was Thomas Hunt Morgan (1866–1945), a Columbia University zoologist interested in studying heredity. Morgan and his colleagues performed a number of experiments with fruit flies (*Drosophila melanogaster*) and became converts to the theory. Morgan discovered sex linkage, in which certain genes were located on the sex chromosomes—the chromosomes that determine the sex of individuals in many species, including humans—and determined that other genes were likewise located at specific sites on other chromosomes. Genes on the same chromosome, whether a sex chromosome or other non-sex chromosome (**autosome**), were said to be linked.

Morgan and his group demonstrated repeatedly that genes on different chromosomes (**unlinked genes**) independently assorted into novel combinations in the offspring. Even so, **linked genes** likewise recombined into novel combinations. They determined that this phenomenon occurred early in meiosis via a process called **synapsis** and crossing over—where the two copies of a chromosome (a **homologous pair**) lined up together and the strands of the maternal chromosome became cross-linked, or entangled, with the strands of the paternal chromosome. As the cell divided in the first division of meiosis, each chromosome acquired a unique mixture of maternal and paternal alleles.

As Morgan pondered his data, he suspected that the farther apart two linked genes were from each other on a chromosome, the more likely they would be to separate during synapsis and crossing over, and the more likely they would not occur together in individual offspring. Morgan began calculating crossover and recombination frequencies among offspring of crossing experiments as a measure of the distance between two genes. One of his students, Alfred Sturtevant (1891–1970), used the frequencies to develop the first genetic, or linkage, map.

Genetic mapping as done with fruit flies does not work well with humans. Aside from ethical considerations involving forced mating between individuals, there are too few humans, overly long generation times—a simple Mendelian-style crossing experiment would take decades to generate F2 results—too many chromosomes, and too many genes to make sense of the data. The key to the answer lay in discovering how genetic information is carried on chromosomes and in developing ways to analyze that information directly.

5

THE LANGUAGE
OF LIFE

In Morgan's day, scientists knew that chromosomes were largely made up of **chromatin**, a complex of two classes of molecules: **proteins** and a poorly understood material called **deoxyribonucleic acid**, or **DNA**. Given that proteins were highly complex molecules made up of repeated units called **amino acids**, they were the front-running candidate for the carrier of genetic information. Some argued, for bacteria at least, that **polysaccharides**—large sugars analogous in complexity and structure to proteins—could carry genetic information.

The answer came in efforts to solve a riddle posed by an experiment conducted by British geneticist Frederick Griffith (1879–1941) in 1928. Griffith was trying to develop a pneumonia vaccine for the British government. He worked with two strains of the *Streptococcus pneumonia* bacterium—a smooth (S) strain that was highly **virulent** and a rough (R) strain that was **avirulent**, or not virulent. Laboratory rats injected with the S strain developed pneumonia and died within days. Rats injected with the R strain remained healthy, as did rats injected with the heat-killed S strain. When rats were injected with a combination of live R strain and dead S strain bacteria, however, they quickly became ill and died. Cultures taken from their bodies revealed only the

S strain. Something had transformed the avirulent bacteria into the virulent form.

During World War II, Oswald Avery (1877–1955), Colin McLeod (1909–1972), and Maclyn McCarty (1911–2005) decided to find out what transformed the bacteria, devising an ingenious experiment to identify the transforming material. They extracted chemical material from S strain *Streptococcus pneumonia* and treated it with chemicals to remove **polysaccharides**. The extract succeeded in transforming the R strain to the S strain. They further treated the extract with trypsin or chymotrypsin, **enzymes** that break down proteins—and the extract was still able to transform the bacteria. They also treated the extract with ribonuclease, an enzyme that breaks down **ribonucleic acid (RNA)** instead of DNA. The extract was still capable of transforming the bacteria. By the process of elimination, neither polysaccharides, proteins, nor RNA could have been the transforming factor. Chemical analysis, however, left one candidate standing—DNA.

Many researchers were reluctant to accept the results of the Avery-McLeod-McCarty experiment, however. Alfred Hershey (1908–1997) and Martha Chase (1923–2003), working with **bacteriophages**—viruses that infect bacteria—firmly settled the question with another ingenious experiment. Bacteriophages are basically a protein coating that surrounds a small amount of DNA inside. They attach to the surface of a bacterium and infect it, forcing it to make more copies of individual **phage** particles. Hershey and Chase used T2, a bacteriophage built like a lunar lander from the Apollo program, and radioactively labeled either the protein coat or the DNA. They allowed the labeled phages to infect bacteria. When phages with labeled protein were used, radioactivity was detected in the protein coats of the old virus particles, but not inside the infected cells. When

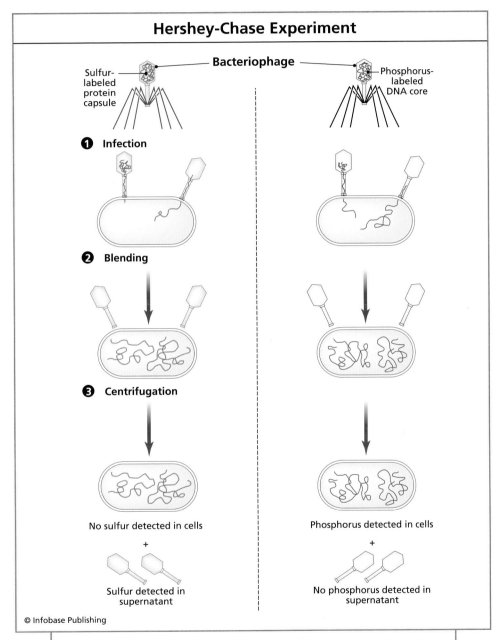

Hershey-Chase Experiment

Sulfur-labeled protein capsule

Bacteriophage

Phosphorus-labeled DNA core

❶ **Infection**

❷ **Blending**

❸ **Centrifugation**

No sulfur detected in cells

+

Sulfur detected in supernatant

Phosphorus detected in cells

+

No phosphorus detected in supernatant

FIGURE 5.1   The Hershey and Chase experiment determined that DNA was the carrier of a cell's genetic material.

phages labeled with radioactive DNA were used, radioactivity was detected inside the bacterial cells, but not in the protein coats of the old virus particles. There could be no doubt afterward that DNA was the primary genetic material.

THE DOUBLE HELIX

The next question to be settled was the structure of DNA, as knowledge of its structure could provide clues to its function. By the late 1940s, a number of researchers had begun trying to find ways to determine it. Among them was Maurice Wilkins (1916–2004), a British physicist who had worked on the Manhattan Project—the effort to build the atomic bomb—during World War II and sought something else to do following his disillusionment after the dropping of the first two products of the project on the cities of Hiroshima and Nagasaki in Japan. He decided to apply his skills to biology, and after taking a job at the Biophysics Research Unit at King's College in London, began—with student Raymond Gosling (b. 1926) using X-ray diffraction images to discern the structure of DNA. By the late spring of 1950, Wilkins and Gosling had taken images of DNA that suggested it had a regular, crystalline structure. Wilkins began talking to a friend of his at Cambridge, Francis Crick (1916–2004), about the importance of DNA. Crick, who had been teaching himself the principles of X-ray crystallography, began applying them to the study of the structure of helical molecules.

The director of the Biophysics Research Unit, Sir John Randall (1905–1984), brought another person over from Laboratoire Central des Services Chimiques de l'État in Paris to help with the DNA work. That person was Rosalind Franklin (1920–1958), an expert in X-ray diffraction. Randall asked her to begin work on DNA—even before she returned to her native England early in 1951. Randall did not discuss

FIGURE 5.2   Rosalind Franklin's work in X-ray crystallography was instrumental in determining the double-helix structure of DNA.

his plans for how she and Wilkins were to work together. Wilkins had begun work on the problem before Franklin and thought she was supposed to assist him. Because she had been asked by Randall to work on it, Franklin thought the problem was hers. She took Gosling and kept the best DNA material for her work. Wilkins, in turn, felt she was poaching his project. Randall did little to clear up any misunderstandings, with dire consequences for his lab later on.

Meanwhile, late in the spring of 1951, Wilkins gave a talk about his work on DNA structure at a seminar in Naples, Italy. An ambitious American researcher, James Watson (b. 1928), who was working as a postdoctoral researcher in Copenhagen, saw the talk and realized from the images Wilkins presented that DNA must have a regular, crystalline structure. He broke off his appointment in Copenhagen and found his way to Cambridge University's Cavendish Lab to be closer to the center of action on DNA research. There he met Crick, and the two began talking to Wilkins about the work.

By then they all knew that the DNA molecule consisted of a long, helical (coiled) chain composed of **nucleotides**, which in turn are made of a five-carbon sugar (**deoxyribose**), a phosphate group, and a **nitrogenous base**. The backbone of the chain consisted of linkages between the phosphate group of one nucleotide and the sugar on the next. The nitrogenous bases turned either inward or outward from the chain. Only four nitrogenous bases were used in DNA, adenine (A), guanine (G), cytosine (C), and thymine (T).

Watson and Crick began a correspondence with Wilkins, who shared his results along with what he knew of Franklin's work—without her knowledge. Watson attended a seminar given by Franklin in November 1951. Among her findings were that the molecule was formed from two, three, or four parallel chains; that the sugar-phosphate backbone was on the outside of the molecule; and a few other details she added that provided clues to the overall structure. (At the time, Franklin disagreed with Wilkins in his conclusion that the molecule was a helix.) Watson had not paid sufficient attention to Franklin's talk; as a result, his notes of the seminar were garbled. He rushed back to Cavendish Lab, and he and Crick quickly put together a model based on his rather

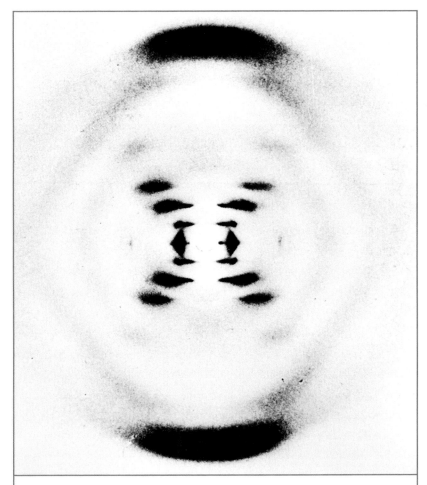

FIGURE 5.3   Photo 51 *(above)* is the famous photo of DNA taken by Rosalind Franklin.

inaccurate notes—a molecule composed of three helices, with the sugar-phosphate backbones on the inside. Prematurely sensing triumph, they invited Wilkins and Franklin over to check out their model. Franklin quickly spotted one major problem: The sugar-phosphate backbones had to be on the outside.

Meanwhile, Franklin, because of her lack of experience with organic molecules, was making little headway in the DNA work. She was also unhappy in the rather chauvinistic environment of King's College and planned to leave for another position early in 1953. In March 1952, she had taken one excellent image of DNA, now famous as Photo 51, but had set it aside as it was taken of a form of the molecule she was not focusing on at the time. Nevertheless, she had by early 1953 come to the conclusion that it was a double helix and made measurements of its width (2 nanometers, or nm) and the distance required for one complete turn of the helix (3.4 nm)—thousands of times thinner than a strand of human hair.

Somehow, Wilkins obtained a copy of Photo 51 and showed it to Watson in early 1953. Crick obtained a copy of an internal progress report on Franklin's research from King's College. (Randall, knowing that Franklin was planning to leave King's College, had by now asked her to end her work on DNA.) Crick and Watson revisited the problem with a renewed sense of urgency. The two were very much worried that the American Linus Pauling (1901–1994) would solve the structure of DNA before they did. They had heard that he had submitted a paper proposing a model of the molecule. Even though it was published before Crick and Watson found the answer, Pauling's model had several major flaws—some of the same mistakes that they had made in their initial attempt at building a model. Pauling had planned to go to England to attend a scientific conference in 1952.

FIGURE 5.4   James Watson (*left*) and Francis Crick examine their model of the structure of DNA many years after they were awarded a Nobel Prize for their work.

If he had, he might have obtained access to the data being generated by Wilkins and Franklin and still won the race to discover the structure of DNA, but his passport was withheld by the U.S. State Department because he was suspected of harboring communist sympathies.

Watson, in attempting to build models of the molecule, continued to put the sugar-phosphate backbone on the inside, but early in February 1953, Crick finally persuaded him to turn things around and put the sugar-phosphate backbone on the outside. Crick had also deduced, from some of Franklin's measurements, that the two strands had to be antiparallel, that is, one strand runs from top to bottom while the adjoining (complementary) strand runs from bottom to top. The next question was how to assemble the two chains in a manner that fit the known dimensions of the molecule. Watson and Crick had learned from Erwin Chargaff (1905–2002) that the amounts of the four nitrogenous bases varied from species to species—but within a species the amounts of adenine always equaled thymine and the amounts of cytosine always equaled guanine. This suggested complementary base pairing: cytosine on one strand of DNA always paired with guanine on the other; likewise, adenine always paired with thymine. Working with paper models, Watson discovered a way to make complementary base pairing work while still maintaining the constant width of the DNA molecule.

In putting their new model together, its elegance was readily apparent. It fit all of the observations. It suggested the ways in which genetic information could be stored—in the sequence of nitrogenous bases—and hinted at how the molecule could replicate itself (one strand serves as a template to make a copy of the other). They completed their new model by March 7, 1953. Watson and Crick quickly wrote a manuscript and submitted it to the British journal *Nature*.

They had offered Wilkins a chance to be a coauthor, but he declined, as he had not been directly involved in the final stages of solving the problem. Instead, negotiations between Director of the Cavendish Lab Sir William Lawrence Bragg, Randall, and the editor of *Nature* resulted in a package of

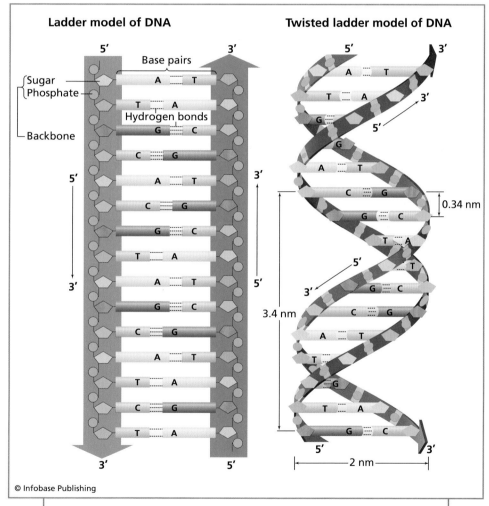

FIGURE 5.5 In a DNA molecule, the double helix structure of nucleotides resembles a ladder whose "rungs" are the nitrogenous base pairs. The base pairs join the strands of DNA together.

related papers appearing in the April 25, 1953, issue of the journal. Watson and Crick's paper on the structure of DNA was first, followed by one by Wilkins (with Alexander Stokes and Herbert Wilson) and another by Franklin and Gosling with supporting X-ray diffraction studies.

A revolution in the biological sciences had begun. Watson, Crick, and Wilkins were awarded the Nobel Prize in Physiology or Medicine in 1962 for their work. Franklin was ineligible for the award at the time—she had died of ovarian cancer in 1958, and Nobel rules prohibit posthumous honors.

THE LANGUAGE OF LIFE

Prior to World War II, substantial evidence had accumulated to suggest that genes—whatever they were—coded for the production of **protein**. After the discovery of the structure of DNA, a race began to determine how genes accomplished this task. Crick pointed the way with something he called the "central dogma" of molecular biology. The dogma is most briefly repeated as "DNA specifies RNA, which specifies protein," and as such is something of an oversimplification, but it was a good guide for those searching for how the information in DNA produces fully functioning organisms.

Proteins are **polypeptides**—molecules made of sequences of amino acids that, once formed, can bend or fold in many ways, and that can bind to other polypeptide units to form large, complex structures. Watson and Crick, in searching the scientific literature, came up with a list of 20 amino acids that could be found in most organisms, and they suspected that something in the sequence of nitrogenous bases in DNA coded in turn for sequences of amino acids.

To get from DNA to protein, a special type of RNA—called **messenger RNA** or **mRNA**—must be synthesized from the template stored in a segment of DNA. (That segment of DNA is what we now call the "gene.") The process of making mRNA is called **transcription**. Complementary base pairing is key to the preservation of information stored in the original, or template, strand of DNA. Complementary base pairing between DNA and RNA is similar to that between strands of DNA. The only difference—since RNA has the nitrogenous base uracil (U) instead of thymine—is that uracil on RNA pairs with adenine.

Once complete, the mRNA strand breaks free of the DNA strand. It is then read as a blueprint by a cellular structure called the **ribosome** (largely made of a second type of RNA, **ribosomal RNA** or **rRNA**), which is responsible for assembling amino acids in the proper order designated by the mRNA. But how?

Many researchers worked to decode the genetic language. How can an almost infinite number of proteins be created from an alphabet with essentially four letters (GCAT in DNA and CGAU in RNA) and only about 20 words (amino acids)? Marshall Nirenberg (b. 1927) and Gobind Khorana (b. 1922) played key roles in deciphering the answers. First, Marianne Grunberg-Manago (b. 1921), a French biochemist, discovered an enzyme in 1955 that could be used to assemble nucleotides into long RNA polymers. With that, Nirenberg and Khorana, in their respective labs, could assemble RNA strands containing specific sequences of nucleotides. On May 15, 1961, Heinrich Matthaei (b. 1929), a researcher in Nirenberg's lab, discovered that strands of RNA containing only uracil coded for the proteins made solely of the amino acid phenylalanine. The Nirenberg and Khorana labs spent the next few years trying to determine the "spelling" of other genetic words, with the process greatly aided by a discovery by Nirenberg and Philip Leder (b. 1934), another researcher in Nirenberg's lab, that the length of the genetic words were only three letters long, such that UUU on mRNA spelled phenylalanine, for example. That discovery, coupled with the knowledge that there are only four nitrogenous bases in RNA, meant that the genetic vocabulary was incredibly simple—there were only 64 possible "words," what biologists call **codons**.

Khorana discovered that three of those codons signaled the end of a polypeptide chain; hence, they were called **stop codons**. Of the remaining 61 codons, only one (AUG) coded for the amino acid methionine (which is always at the front of a polypeptide chain; hence, AUG is also called a start codon), and one (UGG) coded for tryptophan. The other amino acids are coded for by more than one codon—leucine and arginine can be called for by six codons each. Because of the variety of alternate "spellings" for most amino acids, the genetic code is said to be redundant. But since one codon means only one thing, whether an amino acid or the end of a peptide chain, it is also specific.

While Nirenberg, Khorana, and others decoded the genetic language, Robert Holley (1922–1993) discovered a key component in the assembly of proteins from an mRNA template—**transfer RNA, or tRNA**. Transfer RNAs are small molecules that bind to specific amino acids at one end. At the other end, they have a three-nucleotide segment of RNA called an **anticodon**. With the discovery of tRNA and the

---

FIGURE 5.6 *(opposite page)* Messenger RNA (mRNA) is created through transcription. mRNA acts as a messenger, taking DNA's instructions on making proteins and transferring those instructions from the nucleus of the cell to ribosomes, which are structures in the cell's cytoplasm that make protein. In translation, a codon—a group of three mRNA bases—tells which amino acids are needed to make a protein.

decoding of the genetic language, the process of assembling proteins based on the code stored in mRNA—called **translation**—can be explained.

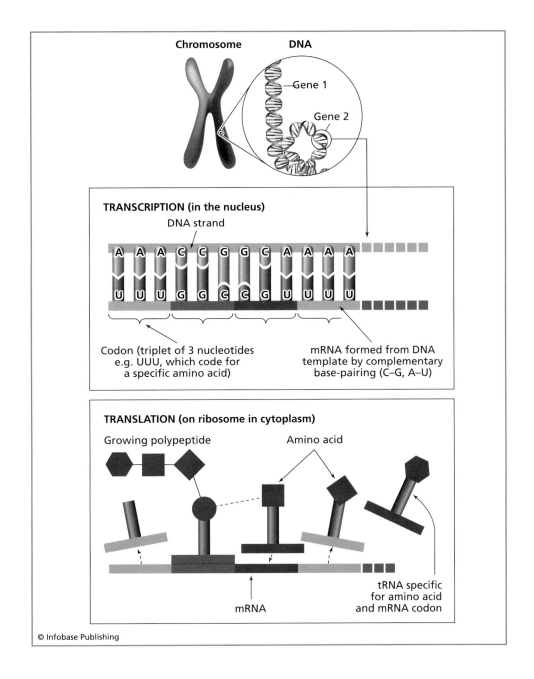

Chromosome   **DNA**

Gene 1

Gene 2

TRANSCRIPTION (in the nucleus)

DNA strand

| A | A | A | C | C | G | G | C | A | A | A | A |

| U | U | U | G | G | C | C | G | U | U | U | U |

Codon (triplet of 3 nucleotides e.g. UUU, which code for a specific amino acid)

mRNA formed from DNA template by complementary base-pairing (C–G, A–U)

TRANSLATION (on ribosome in cytoplasm)

Growing polypeptide   Amino acid

tRNA specific for amino acid and mRNA codon

mRNA

When a strand of mRNA is being "read" by the ribo-some, the anticodon of a tRNA attaches to the codon of the mRNA by complementary base pairing. The first amino acid attached is methionine. Once the tRNA and mRNA are paired, the mRNA is essentially moved down the assembly line of the ribosome until the next codon is in position. Another tRNA, whose anticodon is complementary, pairs with the mRNA. The new amino acid is attached to the methionine. The mRNA moves down the line again, and another amino acid is brought to the ribosome and attached to the end of the growing polypeptide chain. Translation continues until a stop codon is brought to the assembly point; the ribosome then releases both the new polypeptide chain as well as the mRNA. The new polypeptide may undergo further processing, such as being combined with other polypeptide chains, before it becomes a functioning protein.

DAUNTING CHALLENGES

By the one-hundredth anniversary of George Huntington's paper on hereditary chorea, the genetic code had been deciphered, but because of the size of the human **genome**, only a tiny portion of the genetic text had been read. For people working with genetic maladies such as Huntington's disease, techniques had to be developed to locate, isolate, and decode specific genes that may play a role. The key was to break the vast human genome into manageable portions. That key was soon to be found.

6

THE MOLECULAR HUNT BEGINS

For someone with a parent afflicted by Huntington's disease, the first few decades of life could be filled with fear. The disease gave no advance warning that one might be destined to die of it, nor did it offer any solace that one could live worry free. All a person could do was wait, take care of the affected parent, and hope and/or pray that one might escape the parent's destiny. Some coped with the possibility quite well; others lived in dread—even to the point of committing suicide when symptoms of the disease began to manifest themselves.

The discovery of DNA and the decryption of the genetic code offered hope a genetic marker could be found that could provide either advance warning or lifelong relief. Given the scope of the human genome and the large number of chromosomes that might harbor the allele that triggered the disease, the marker would not be easy to find. Studies based on pedigree analysis offered some clues, but failed to narrow the field much.

A FAMILY THING

At the turn of the twentieth century, Americans were enthusiastically developing pedigrees of their families—often in

65

search of illustrious ancestors that could fuel pretensions to prominence. For researchers of diseases that appeared to run in families, pedigree analysis—together with an understanding of Mendel's findings in genetics—could provide evidence that might confirm a genetic link as well as provide evidence for how the disease is passed on.

For much of the nineteenth century, Huntington's disease and Sydenham's chorea were frequently confused under the banner of St. Vitus's dance prior to the recognition that they are two different diseases. Some experts thought Sydenham's chorea could be inherited, as Huntington's disease was. After the link between Sydenham's chorea and rheumatic fever was established, however, researchers realized the apparent "inheritance" pattern of Sydenham's chorea was merely a clustering of family members who had the bacterial infection that caused rheumatic fever and were therefore at risk of developing Sydenham's chorea.

In the case of Huntington's disease, people in the areas where it occurred often realized it ran in families. For example, on the morning of June 11, 1806—just a few years after Abel Huntington moved to East Hampton—Captain David Hedges awoke in his home to find that his 42-year-old wife, Phebe (nee Tillinghast), was missing. A search ensued, and the searchers traced her footsteps for a mile from the Hedges's home to the shore of the Atlantic Ocean. Days later, her body was found washed up onshore near Montauk, about 20 miles (32 kilometers) east of where she had disappeared. The Hedges were wealthy and held in high esteem by the community. Phebe had all the usual reasons to be happy, so initially the reason for her suicidal walk was a mystery. A report later that month in the *Suffolk Gazette*, however, offered an answer: "This extraordinary step is attributed to her extreme dread of the disorder called *St. Vitus' dance*, with which she began to be affected, and which her mother has to a great degree."[16]

Phebe Hedges (1764–1806) was the daughter of Captain John Tillinghast and Phebe Mulford (1739–1811). As the *Sag Harbor Gazette* story suggested, her mother was already afflicted by the disease. Captain Tillinghast and his wife had two other daughters, Nancy (1777–1807) and Lydia (1777–1870). Lydia Tillinghast's first son, Edmund, was born out of wedlock. Lydia later married William Bennett (d. 1809), with whom she had a son, William (1807–1856). Neither Lydia nor her sons nor her grandchildren were afflicted by Huntington's disease.

Descendants of Phebe and Nancy were not as lucky. Phebe had two sons, Stafford (1786–1833) and Stephen (1790–1875), and a daughter, Betsy (1795–1821). Betsy Hedges married Squires Miller and died quite young—too early to develop symptoms of the disease. Her son, Squires H. Miller, married, but little is known about his life. Stephen Hedges, who married Esther Miller, did not develop the disease, and neither did his children. Stafford Hedges, who married Nancy Baker, developed the disease, as did two of his four children, Phebe Hedges (1809–1868) and Hiram Baker Hedges (1820–c.1861).

Nancy Tillinghast, who married Elisha Payne, was also afflicted by the disease. She had seven children. Little is known of the fate of six of her children, but one, Elias Payne (1812–c.1870), is known to have developed Huntington's disease. Elias married Betsy Miller. Two of his six children, Nancy Elizabeth (1834–1890) and Albert Madison (1838–1899), were likewise afflicted by Huntington's disease.

PATTERNS OF INHERITANCE

Even though Mendel's work was not widely known at the time Huntington published his landmark paper in 1872—and even though his paper was not yet published at the time that

Elliotson, Waters, Lyon, Gorman, and Lund had published their work—each of these physicians had, by compiling and analyzing pedigrees of afflicted families, discerned the basic patterns of inheritance of the disease. One of the most striking facts was that the disease, unlike some other hereditary disorders, did not skip generations. George Huntington and the others who described hereditary chorea, in reviewing such family data, noticed that the disease almost never occurred in an individual whose parent did not also have the disease. Later researchers found rare exceptions, such as instances wherein an individual's parent had been afflicted with the disease, but died too young to develop symptoms. An example is that of Lewis "P," of Stratford, Connecticut. His father, Charles, and daughter, Harriett, both were stricken by Huntington's disease. Lewis, however, was killed in the Civil War at the age of 25. (Another exception to this rule, to be discussed later, is when a **mutation** triggers the disease in a person with no family history of it.)

Recessive traits might not appear for several generations, persisting invisibly in the genetic line of a family until a child inherits a copy of the recessive allele from both parents. Since Huntington's disease rarely skips generations, it could not be a recessive trait. If a person carried just one copy of the allele that triggers the disease, he or she would be afflicted by it—as long as the person lived long enough to develop symptoms.

Sex chromosomes differentiate male from female. In humans, the sex chromosomes are denoted as either X or Y. Females have two X chromosomes; males have an X and a Y chromosome. The sex of the individual is determined by whether the sperm cell that fertilizes an egg to form a new individual carries the X or the Y chromosome. A **sex-linked trait**—that is, a trait whose gene is located on one of the sex chromosomes—may pass unnoticed through several generations of females if it is carried on the X chromosome and if it is recessive. A female would have to carry a copy of the recessive allele on each X chromosome to express (have) the trait. A male child who inherits the X chromosome from his mother would express the trait if his mother passed the recessive allele along with it. (A sex-linked trait carried on the Y chromosome would only be seen in males, and since males normally have only one Y chromosome, the concept of dominant versus recessive makes little sense.) Huntington's disease, since it occurs in females (Phebe Hedges) as well as males, cannot be carried on the Y chromosome. Since men could inherit the disease from their fathers (Phebe Hedges's grandson Hiram Baker Hedges inherited the disease from her son Stafford), and since some, but not all daughters could inherit the disease from their father (Stafford Hedges passed the disease on to his daughter Phebe, but not to his other daughter, Margaret), the gene likewise cannot be carried on the X chromosome—men inherit only a Y chromosome from their fathers, and fathers pass on only one X chromosome to their daughters.

Ruling out sex linkage narrowed the field somewhat, but not much. That left any of 22 pairs of autosomes (non-sex chromosomes) as the place where the gene that causes Huntington's disease lay hidden. If people with a family history of Huntington's disease were to do more than wait to develop symptoms before learning that they, too, had the disease, researchers were going to have to sift through a vast swath of the human genome to find a marker that could provide advance warning. Narrowing the search would be difficult because of (1) the relatively late age of onset of the disease, and (2) the relatively small number of individuals that could serve as study subjects.

Researchers searched through **karyotypes**—images of the full complement of chromosomes, usually stained with

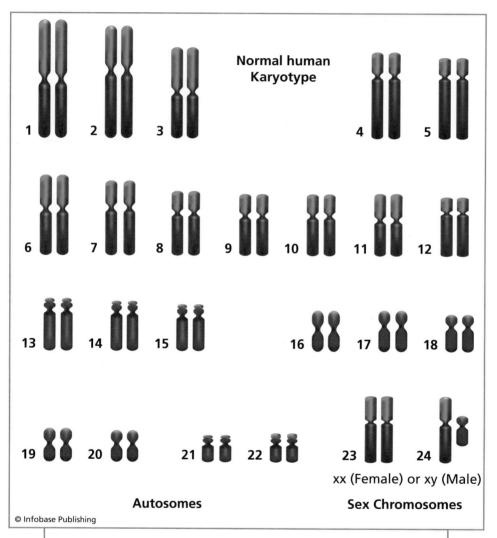

Normal human Karyotype

1 2 3 4 5
6 7 8 9 10 11 12
13 14 15 16 17 18
19 20 21 22 23 24

xx (Female) or xy (Male)

Autosomes   Sex Chromosomes

© Infobase Publishing

FIGURE 6.1 A normal human karyotype shows all 23 pairs of chromosomes.

some kind of dye or labeled with some kind of marker (such as radioactive tracers) and ordered in homologous pairs sorted from the longest pair of autosomes to the shortest, followed by the sex chromosomes. They looked for any chromosomal abnormalities that might explain the disease. Possible abnormalities include chromosomes that are missing parts, chromosomes with excess parts, chromosomes that should be separate but are joined together, too many or too few copies of a specific chromosome, or abnormal stain or marker patterns. No obvious chromosomal defect could be found.

Researchers needed literally to break the genome down into manageable chunks, and by 1971 a way to do so had been found.

MOLECULAR KNIVES

Early in the 1950s, when James Watson and Francis Crick were racing to crack the genetic code, two sets of researchers studying the replication of viruses—Salvador E. Luria (1912–1991) and Mary L. Human, and Giuseppe Bertani and Jean-Jacques Weigle (1901–1968)—noticed that in some cases the viruses, after infecting one strain of host bacteria, were modified in ways that limited their abilities to reproduce in other strains of bacteria. The researchers ruled out some kind of natural selection process, as the changes occurred within a single growth cycle of the viruses. Something within the host bacteria restricted viral growth. Werner Arber (b. 1928) suggested that a chemical agent was responsible—an enzyme. By the end of the 1960s, he and other researchers had found enzymes that bound to specific DNA sequences and snipped the DNA strands. Unfortunately, these enzymes snipped the DNA at some distance from the recognition site, regardless of the DNA sequence at the cutting site. As a result, they proved unsuitable for mapping the genome and discovering specific genetic markers within it. What was needed was something that would cut DNA at a specific location.

The solution to the problem was accidentally discovered in the laboratory of Hamilton O. Smith (b. 1931) at the end of the 1960s. Smith and his colleagues were using the bacterium *Haemophilus influenzae* as an incubator for the bacteriophage *Salmonella* phage P22, which they happened to be studying. (Viruses require a host cell for replication, as they lack the ability to reproduce themselves.) The phage DNA was radioactively labeled. After giving the virus appropriate time to replicate, Smith and his colleagues analyzed the bacterial cells but found no trace of its DNA. The bacterial DNA, however, was intact. Something inside the bacteria had destroyed the viral DNA.

Smith and his coworkers, K.W. Wilcox and Thomas J. Kelly Jr., discovered an **endonuclease**—an enzyme that splits nucleic acid chains, that is, a **restriction enzyme**—that cleaved the viral DNA but took no action against the bacterial DNA. This endonuclease split the DNA at a specific nucleotide sequence.

```
5'    GT | AC   3'
3'    CA | TG   5'
```

Smith and Wilcox referred to a break such as the one above as an "even" break. As more restriction enzymes were discovered, many were found to cause what Smith and Wilcox called "staggered" breaks. For example, the following sequence is symmetrical, that is, one strand is a mirror image of the other.

```
5'  ATATCGAGATAT   3'
3'  TATAGCTCTATA   5'
```

A staggered break would sever the strands at corresponding sites on each strand.

```
5'  ATAT | CGAGATAT  3'
3'  TATAGCTC | TATA   5'
```

The result would be unpaired ends, otherwise known as "sticky" ends, which will readily bind to a complementary nucleotide sequence.

```
5'  ATAT   CGAGATAT  3'
3'  TATAGCTC   TATA   5'
```

Genetic engineers today take advantage of such sticky ends to insert foreign genes into the chromosomes of other organisms, such as inserting a human insulin gene into a yeast chromosome so the genetically modified yeast can be used to safely and relatively inexpensively make large amounts of the hormone that diabetics need to help regulate sugar levels in their bloodstream. Markers can likewise be inserted to "tag" specific portions of a chromosome for later identification.

Smith had made a major discovery—worthy of Nobel Prize recognition—but the technique he used to separate the DNA fragments created by restriction enzymes, what we now call **restriction fragments**, was too crude to be of much use in applications such as DNA marker identification and genetic mapping. Smith took the DNA that had been treated with the restriction enzyme and subjected subsets of the material to **centrifugation** (essentially spinning) for five minutes in sucrose solutions ranging from 5% sucrose to 20% sucrose. The greater the sucrose concentration, the greater the resistance to movement of the larger restriction fragments. By being limited to using fixed increments in concentration, the resolution of the procedure—its ability to differentiate between restriction fragments that were slightly different in size—limited the ability of the procedure to differentiate segments of DNA.

GEL ELECTROPHORESIS

Smith's friend, Daniel Nathans (1928–1999), whose lab was next door, thought another technique might provide better results. **Gel electrophoresis** had been used for several decades to separate molecular components of a mixture. In many ways it was analogous to the paper chromatography experiments done in many high school and college classrooms. In paper chromatography, a mixture such as ink can be separated into its components as they are dissolved in a solvent and wicked up by a piece of paper. The solvent evaporates as it moves up the paper away from its source; the dissolved components are left in more or less distinct bands on the paper, separated according to their solubility—more soluble components move farther up the paper than less soluble ones.

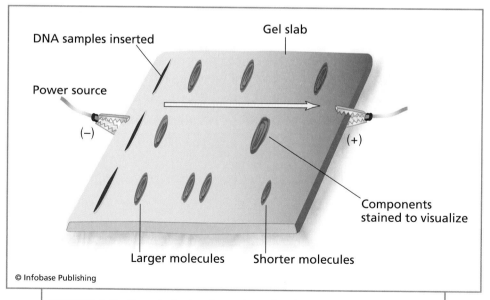

FIGURE 6.2 In gel electrophoresis, scientists use porous gels and an electrical current to separate the molecular components of a mixture into order based on their size.

Instead of using paper and solvents, gel electrophoresis uses porous gels (which can be made of various materials) and electrical current to separate the components of a mixture. The mixture is placed into small wells at one end of a thin slab of gel. At the time that Nathans first experimented with gel electrophoresis, the gels were not formed into thin slabs; instead, they were housed inside vertical Plexiglas tubing. The gel is then immersed in an aqueous (water) solution, and an electrical current is passed through the solution via electrodes inserted at either end. With the current on, the components move through the pores in the gel. The distance they travel is a function of size, the amount of electrical charge, and other characteristics; the direction they move is a function of whether their net electrical charge is positive or negative. Positively charged components move in the direction of the negative electrode; negatively charged components move in the direction of the positive one. Since nucleic acids and nucleic acid fragments are negatively charged, because of the phosphate groups that make up their backbone, they move toward the positive electrode. The primary factor controlling the separation of the nucleic acid components was their size—smaller fragments would move more easily through the pores, thus traveling farther in a given amount of time.

In 1967, Ulrich Loening published the results of a test of gel electrophoresis to see how well it could separate rRNA components. The gels—in this case, polyacrylamide gels—could be made with different pore sizes. As a result, one could select a pore size appropriate for detecting whatever material was of interest. Loening found that gel electrophoresis allowed for more precise separation of nucleic acids than the density gradient techniques, such as the one used by Smith. He also found that they could be used to analyze a large number of samples quickly, and that, after the gel was removed from the solution, or tubing in Loening's case, it could easily be examined in other ways, such as under ultraviolet light, to make it easier to compare and contrast results.

Kathleen Danna, who worked in Nathans's lab, did a quick test to see how well gel electrophoresis could separate fragments of radioactively labeled simian virus 40 DNA that had been treated with Smith's restriction enzyme. After the gels were developed, she removed one set from the glass tubes, sliced them, and laid them on an unexposed X-ray film. The images that resulted were banded—the bands revealing the locations of radioactively labeled DNA segments. Another set of gels was sliced into segments; each segment was passed through a **scintillation counter** to measure the amount of DNA the segment contained. The **autoradiographs** were better able to resolve individual bands. Danna

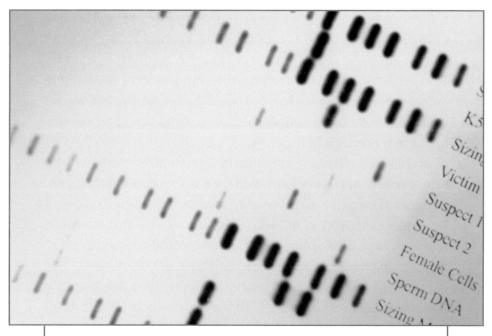

FIGURE 6.3   Restriction fragment analysis can be used to compare DNA from different individuals.

and Nathans compared DNA segment length measurements obtained from the autoradiographs, the scintillation counter data, and from direct measurements obtained from an electron microscope to make sure that each method yielded results consistent with the other two techniques.

Danna and Nathans saw great potential for restriction fragment analysis (1) to map the genome, (2) to identify areas where DNA was being replicated, (3) to identify when certain segments of DNA are transcribed, (4) to identify the location of specific genes by testing for biological activity, (5) to create useful mutants by deleting one or more targeted fragments, and (6) to find differences in specific DNA segments among different individuals or species. Nathans's research group wasted little time in trying to prove the predictions. Over the next few years, they and their collaborators published papers that fulfilled each prediction. Arber, Nathans, and Smith shared the Nobel Prize in Physiology or Medicine in 1978 for the discovery of "restriction enzymes and their application to problems of molecular genetics."

RESTRICTION FRAGMENT ANALYSIS

In discussing differences in DNA segments among individuals or species, Danna and Nathans offered a key observation: "Comparison of restriction endonuclease digests by polyacrylamide gel electrophoresis has also provided a new method for detecting differences in DNA. By this means, we have found that the DNA of small-plaque, large-plaque, and minute-plaque SV40 strains show specific differences in the mobility of particular DNA fragments."[17]

The differences in mobility of the "particular DNA fragments" resulted from differences in size of particular segments—restriction fragments—of the genome. For example, a researcher has applied a restriction enzyme to DNA from three individuals. For one chromosome, four fragments were obtained, and the fragment lengths measured for all three individuals. The data are presented below.

Fragment	Subject		
	A	B	C
1	54	54	54
2	72	72	78
3	117	102	102
4	33	33	33

For all three study subjects, lengths for fragments 1 and 4 are identical. For fragment 2, the length for one subject is 78. For the other two subjects, the length is 72. For fragment 3, the length for one subject is 117. For the other two, the length is 102. The differences in length for fragments 2 and 3 are called **restriction fragment length polymorphisms**, or **RFLPs**.

RFLPs are important in that they can serve as genetic markers that can be used to detect disease-causing genes. Huntington's disease researchers quickly realized their potential.

7

FLAWED GENE, DEADLY PROTEIN

In 1972, Nancy S. Wexler (b. 1945), a clinical psychologist turned Huntington's disease gene hunter, learned of the work of Americo Negrette (1924–2003). Negrette, a Venezuelan physician, discovered a large cluster of families living along the shores of Lake Maracaibo in which an affliction called *el mal* (the bad) ran rampant. People with the affliction were called *sanviteros.* Negrette determined that it was actually Huntington's disease, which was so prevalent that as many as half the people in some towns in the region were at risk of developing the disease. He began a lifetime of research on the disease, compiling hundreds of pedigrees documenting the inheritance patterns of Huntington's in the region. Wexler, who herself was at risk of developing the disease, visited the region in 1979 and began a long series of annual visits to the region to build upon Negrette's pioneering work. By 1983, a pedigree containing more than 3,000 individuals had been compiled, and all patients with Huntington's disease in the region could be traced to a common ancestor. Wexler also collected tissue samples and clinical data. Wexler and her group had also collected similar pedigree and clinical information and tissues samples from a much smaller American family with Huntington's disease. The tissue samples from the two groups were used

THE COUNTRY DOCTOR: AMERICO NEGRETTE

Americo Negrette (1924–2003), a doctor, biochemist, artist, and poet, grew up in La Cañada, an impoverished district in Venezuela. After his father disappeared during the regime of dictator Juan Vincente Gomez, his mother worked hard to ensure her son got a good education. Inspired by his local doctor, Goyo Boscán, he trained to become a physician himself.

After receiving his degree, Negrette worked as a district physician. His first assignment (1950–1952) was in a town called Palmarejo, where he worked with a boy suffering from epileptic dementia who was convinced only holy water could stop his seizures. Negrette worked with the boy, slowly convincing him to take medications without undermining the boy's faith. Negrette later wrote of his experiences in the town, "We mutually learned many things . . . I taught them about health and they taught me humanity."[18]

Negrette's next assignment was in the town of San Francisco, a rural suburb of Maracaibo. Shortly after his arrival, he

to develop cell cultures that could provide genetic material for the search for the Huntington's disease gene. The genetic material played a decisive role in the gene's discovery.

Geneticist James F. Gusella, who was pioneering the technique of using genetic markers to detect disease genes, first applied the technique to the material from the American family. First, the researchers "digested" the human chromosomes with restriction enzyme HindIII. The fragments were separated via gel electrophoresis. The gels in turn were subjected to Southern blotting—a technique developed by E.M. Southern in which the DNA fragments in the gels are

had a life-changing experience. Negrette later told a colleague: "I arrived in San Francisco, having been transferred from Palmarejo. Some two days after my arrival, I saw a boy staggering through the streets. He fell; stopped and fell again. It bothered me to see this drunk boy, and I commented to my friend what a pity to see such a young boy in such a drunken state."[19]

Negrette's companion replied, "He is not drunk, doctor, he is a *sanvitero*."[20]

Curious about the disorder, Negrette traveled to La Guajira, the village where the boy and others similarly afflicted lived, and began a lifetime of sometimes controversial (but eventually vindicated) research into Huntington's disease. Nancy S. Wexler, who followed in Negrette's footsteps, has built upon the pedigrees he began collecting and has collected data for more than 18,000 persons in the region that have been affected by the disease.

Negrette's pioneering work helped make the discovery of the genetic defect that causes Huntington's disease possible.

transferred (blotted) to a nitrocellulose or nylon membrane. In the process, the DNA is **denatured**, or separated into single strands that can bind to markers specific to certain nucleotide sequences. If a nitrocellulose membrane is used, it is baked to permanently bind the DNA fragments to the membrane. If a nylon membrane is used, the binding is triggered by exposing the membrane to ultraviolet light.

The membrane containing the DNA fragments is then immersed in solution containing markers that feature short stretches of DNA that can hybridize—bind—with restriction fragments made of complementary sequences of DNA. Once the hybridization is complete, the blot can be imaged—often the markers are labeled with radioactive isotopes, so some form of autoradiography can often be used. Visible bands on the image indicate restriction fragments containing segments that correspond with the marker sequence.

Gusella and his colleagues tested a number of markers, but only one, derived from bacteriophage clone G8, showed any potential linkage with Huntington's disease. They tested their findings on the larger Venezuelan sample, in which they also found an association of G8 with the Huntington's disease. The next step was to find the chromosome where the linkage occurred. For that, Gusella and his colleagues turned to human-mouse **somatic cell hybrids**.

Somatic cell hybrids can reveal the location of specific genes by taking advantage of chromosome loss that occurs in cell lines created by the fusion of cells from two different species—a species whose genome is being studied (in this case, humans) and another species whose cells have been genetically modified in some manner that affects growth. This could be accomplished, for example, by eliminating the ability to produce an essential enzyme. The genetic modifications can be tailored so that different strains of the modified cells lack different enzymes—thus, the hybrid can only survive if it contains a chromosome from the species of interest that produces the otherwise missing protein. For example, if trying to detect whether a gene is located on human chromosomes 5, 6, or 7, a researcher would create three modified mouse cell lines, E, F, and G—line E requires an enzyme produced by chromosome 5, line F requires an enzyme produced by chromosome 6, and line G requires an enzyme produced by chromosome 7. The cell mixtures are cultured in a medium that will not support the growth of either parental (pure human or pure mouse) cell line. The hybrid cells, however, survive, and the culture is maintained until maximum chromosome loss is achieved. For example, with a hybrid made from mouse line F, it would be cultured until all human chromosomes but chromosome 6 remain. The surviving hybrids can then be subjected to further analysis, such as treatment by restriction enzymes followed by gel electrophoresis and Southern blotting, to see if the gene of interest is present.

FINDING THE MARKER

The Huntington's disease research team, now called the Huntington's Disease Collaborative Research Group (formed in 1984), analyzed their human-mouse hybrids and found that the G8 marker did not bind to mouse DNA. They determined that whenever human chromosome 4 was present in the hybrid cells, the G8 marker could be found. When human chromosome 4 was missing, the G8 marker would be missing, too. The location of the Huntington's disease gene had been found.

The G8 segment of chromosome 4 was designated D4S10. The discovery laid the foundation for developing a relatively simple test to determine whether someone was at risk of developing the disease. It also had immediate and practical implications for Huntington's researchers—they knew where to focus their efforts in cloning and mapping the gene.

In a karyotype, chromosome 4 looks like a lanky X with long legs and short arms. In subsequent research on individuals with Wolf-Hirschhorn syndrome—a birth defect characterized by mental retardation, microcephaly (abnormally small head), and seizures, among other symptoms, that is caused by a deletion of the tip of the short arm of chromosome 4, including the marker D4S10—the members of the research group deduced that the gene responsible for the disease must be nearby. By 1991, the location of the gene had been pinpointed to band 4p16.3—the terminal band on the short arm of chromosome 4.

Now that they knew where to look on chromosome 4 for the Huntington's disease gene, the Huntington's Disease Collaborative Research Group set out in 1991 to isolate and map it. Even though they were looking in a small area, they faced a major challenge—human DNA is loaded with sequences that do not code for either proteins or other functional RNA. Some of these noncoding stretches regulate activity of specific genes; some have no known purpose. To complicate matters further, some of the noncoding sequences are within genes. The parts of a gene that code for proteins are called **exons;** the parts that do not code for proteins are called **introns**. What the team needed was something that could quickly find the coding sequences in a gene. The technique they chose was a new technique called **exon amplification**, devised by a research team led by Alan Buckler.

Exon amplification works by isolating DNA fragments of interest and inserting them into an intron on a **plasmid**—a bit of circular DNA that can be inserted into a host cell such as yeast. If exons are present, functional mRNA is produced that contains only the coding sequence. The mRNA can then be isolated and amplified by an RNA-based polymerase chain reaction (PCR). The process begins with the reverse of transcription—instead of making mRNA from DNA, complementary DNA (or cDNA) is made from the mRNA with the aid of an enzyme called **reverse transcriptase**. This cDNA is a great improvement over the original DNA fragments in that it contains nothing but coding sequences—not a mix of exons and introns. The cDNA is then subjected to PCR, a process invented by Kary B. Mullis (b. 1944) in 1983, which amplifies DNA exponentially. Mullis's invention was based on observations of DNA repair by Gobind Khorana and others in 1971.

NANCY WEXLER: THE GENE HUNTER

Nancy Sabin Wexler had no plans to become a gene hunter. She took only one biology class in her entire college career—an introductory biology class at Radcliffe College—eventually earning a Ph.D. in clinical psychology in 1974.

Wexler's interest in Huntington's disease was personal. Her mother, Lenore (nee Sabin) Wexler, was diagnosed with the disease in 1968. By that time, the disease had already claimed her maternal grandfather and three uncles. Nancy's mother died little more than 10 years after her diagnosis. Both Nancy Wexler and her sister, Alice Wexler, knew that they, too, were at risk of developing the disease.

After her mother's diagnosis in 1968, Nancy's father, Milton Wexler, established the Hereditary Disease Foundation.

(continues)

Building upon the work started by Americo Negrette, Nancy Wexler studied pedigrees of families with a history of Huntington's disease from the region around Lake Maracaibo, Venezuela.

(continued)

Nancy became president of the foundation in 1969. Her doctoral research at the University of Michigan focused on characteristics of people with the disease. She quickly rose to prominence within the Huntington's disease research community.

Wexler first learned of the work of Americo Negrette in Venezuela in 1972. She visited the Lake Maracaibo region in 1979 and began a long-term research project consisting of annual visits to the region. She and her colleagues have since amassed pedigrees with medical history information for more than 18,000 individuals in the region. Thousands of tissue samples have been collected as well for genetic analysis. The work, begun by Negrette and continued by Wexler, eventually led to the discovery of the gene that causes Huntington's disease.

The work by Wexler and her colleagues has paid off. In addition to Huntington's disease, the research has led to the discovery of genes that cause familial Alzheimer's disease, kidney cancer, neurofibromatosis, amyotrophic lateral sclerosis (Lou Gehrig's disease), and dwarfism.

Mullis followed in Khorana's footsteps by winning the Nobel Prize in Chemistry in 1993 for the invention of PCR.

PCR can begin with a single strand of DNA or with a double-stranded molecule that is denatured by heating. After denaturing is complete, the solution is cooled, allowing primers complementary to the individual strands to bind to one end and begin the replication process. DNA polymerases fill in the rest by adding complementary nucleotides, first at the end of the primer segment, then at the end of the new DNA strand in the proper order, ultimately producing a double-stranded molecule that is an exact copy of the original. The process of heating and denaturing, followed by cooling and replication, can be repeated over and over, increasing the amount of target DNA exponentially. While there are limits to how many copies can be made before copy quality declines, a large number of high-quality copies can be produced in a matter of hours.

As a result of the exon amplification work, the Huntington's Disease Collaborative Research Group was able to isolate and sequence four genes in the 4p16.3 segment of human chromosome 4. Three genes had no abnormalities that could be linked with Huntington's disease. The fourth gene, IT15, however, coded for a previously unknown protein and featured a stretch of repetitive three-base sections (**trinucleotides**) in the sequence CAG (cytosine, adenine, and guanine, which codes for the amino acid glutamine). The CAG repeats were located at the 5′ end—more or less the front—of the gene. Their samples obtained from people without Huntington's disease featured anything from 11 to 34 CAG repeats. Their samples from people with Huntington's disease ranged from 42 to more than 66 repeats. The group also found that the age of onset of disease symptoms was correlated with the number of repeats—the greater the number of repeats, the earlier symptoms manifested themselves. The group had found its quarry. IT15 was the Huntington's disease gene. The group named the protein product of the gene "huntingtin."

HUNTINGTIN

Huntingtin (Htt) is a medium-size protein, containing 3,144 amino acids, and is about 348 kilodaltons (kD) in size. One **dalton** is about equal to the mass of one proton or neutron in an atom. Expressed by cells throughout the body, both inside and outside the nervous system, huntingtin is most

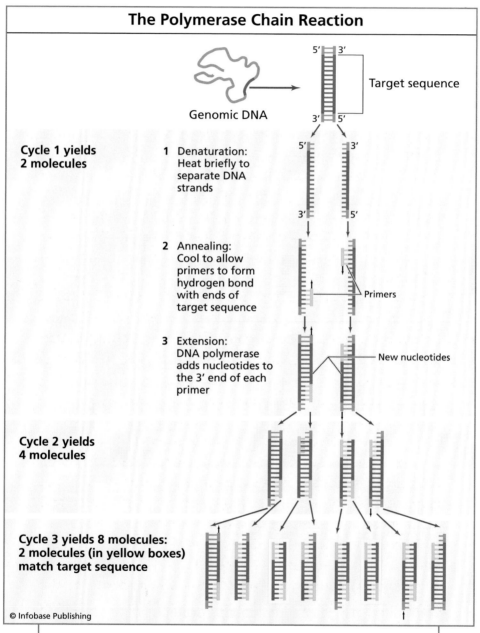

The Polymerase Chain Reaction

Genomic DNA

Target sequence

**Cycle 1 yields
2 molecules**

1 Denaturation:
Heat briefly to
separate DNA
strands

2 Annealing:
Cool to allow
primers to form
hydrogen bond
with ends of
target sequence

Primers

3 Extension:
DNA polymerase
adds nucleotides to
the 3' end of each
primer

New nucleotides

**Cycle 2 yields
4 molecules**

**Cycle 3 yields 8 molecules:
2 molecules (in yellow boxes)
match target sequence**

© Infobase Publishing

FIGURE 7.2 The polymerase chain reaction can quickly amplify a small amount of DNA from a sample into an amount large enough to analyze with other molecular techniques.

highly expressed in the central nervous system (brain and spinal cord) and testes (organs that produce sperm in males). Wild-type (non-disease-causing) huntingtin promotes the survival of nerve cells. Among other things, it protects them from **apoptosis** (programmed cell death) in response to toxic or other adverse stimuli. For example, the protein protects nerve cells from **excitotoxicity**—cell damage and death resulting from overstimulation by excitatory neurotransmitters (chemicals that transmit signals between adjacent nerve cells). If there is no way to clear or block the neurotransmitter from the synapse (the gap between nerve cells where signals are transmitted from one cell to the other), the receiving cell essentially withers and dies from overwork. Huntingtin also promotes the production and transport of **brain-derived neurotrophic factor (BDNF)**, a protein that enhances growth and development, as well as health and survival, of brain cells. Wild-type huntingtin also helps counteract the effects of mutant (disease-causing) huntingtin.

Huntingtin is essential for proper embryonic development. Early in embryonic development, the protein is needed to keep the embryo alive. The wild-type or mutant forms seem to be equally effective. The protein is also necessary later in embryonic development for proper formation of the neural tube—the structure that gives rise to the brain and spinal cord. Again, either type functions equally well.

The key to whether one develops Huntington's disease later in life lies in the region of the CAG repeats—called the polyglutamine or polyQ region—which begin at the eighteenth amino acid in the huntingtin chain. If a person has 35 or fewer repeats, the person is considered "normal" in that there is no risk of developing the disease. Those with more than 35 repeats are at risk of developing the disease. The extent of risk is defined as **penetrance**. A person who has 40 or more repeats is considered to be "fully penetrant"—destined to develop the disease unless he or she dies "prematurely" of some other cause. Those with 36 to 39 repeats have "reduced penetrance"—they may or may not become afflicted with the disease. Length of the repeat is correlated with age of onset of the disease. The longer the repeat is, the earlier symptoms appear. There is no relationship, however, between number of repeats and progression of the illness.

OTHER TRINUCLEOTIDE REPEAT DISORDERS

Currently, there are nearly two dozen diseases believed to be caused by **trinucleotide repeats**. Some are polyglutamine repeat disorders, such as Huntington's disease; some are repeats of other amino acids; and some are caused by trinucleotide repeats in non-protein-coding portions of the genome. A few of the **trinucleotide repeat disorders** are listed below.

Fragile X Syndrome. Fragile X syndrome is caused by CGG repeats in an untranslated region of the FMR1 gene, located on the long arm of the X chromosome. The region normally has 6 to 60 repeats. The disease reaches full penetrance with more than 200 repeats. It is X-linked dominant and is more common in males than in females. Symptoms are likewise more serious in males and are characterized by moderate-to-severe mental retardation, delays in speech development, behavioral and social problems, and physical abnormalities such as enlarged testicles and ears and hyperextensible joints.

Friedreich's Ataxia. Friedreich's **ataxia** is an autosomal recessive disorder caused by a GAA repeat on a noncoding region of the FRDA gene on chromosome 9. The region normally features

The **expansion mutations** that increase the length of the repeat appear to occur in germ-line cells—cells that give rise to sex cells. Typically, they occur during mitosis, the process in which a parent cell divides into two (usually) genetically identical daughter cells, but the mutations may occur during meiosis. Mutation rate appears to be related to the number of somatic cell repeats. The more CAG repeats in the IT15 gene that a person normally has, the more likely he or she is to produce germ-line cells with an increased

6 to 32 repeats. Symptoms appear when there are 200 to 1,700 repeats. It results in ataxia—coordination problems—caused by damage to the spinal cord, brain stem, cerebral cortex, and peripheral nerves. Other symptoms include cardiomyopathy (loss of function in cardiac muscle fibers) and diabetes.

Myotonic Dystrophy. Myotonic dystrophy is caused by CTG repeats on the DMPK gene on chromosome 19. Normally featuring 5 to 37 repeats, 50 to 10,000 repeats causes the disease. Symptoms include **myopathy** (loss of function in muscle fibers), weakness, cataracts, testicular atrophy, and mental retardation.

Spinobulbar Muscular Atrophy. Spinobulbar muscular atrophy (also known as Kennedy's disease) is caused by CAG repeats on the **androgen** receptor gene on the X chromosome. The gene normally has 9 to 36 repeats; in the disease, there are 38 to 62 repeats. Symptoms of this X-linked recessive disorder—which primarily affects males—include muscle weakness and wasting, slowed reflexes, difficulty speaking and swallowing, and sterility.

number of repeats. These expansion mutations are more likely to occur in males than in females. Some research suggests that the nucleotide sequence between the polyglutamine repeat region and a subsequent trinucleotide repeat region (called the polyproline region because it consists of CCG repeats, which code for proline) may influence the likelihood of expansion mutations.

The effects of Huntington's disease may be subject to **genomic imprinting**. In genomic imprinting, the way an allele is expressed is affected by the parent from which the allele is inherited. In other words, the effects of an allele inherited from the father may differ from the effects of that allele if it was inherited from the mother. In Huntington's disease, age of onset, in particular, appears to be subject to genomic imprinting. If the mutant allele is inherited from the mother, the number of CAG repeats in the allele inherited from the father may modify the age of onset. The relationship between trinucleotide repeats on the normal paternal allele and age of onset is inverse—the greater the number of repeats on the paternal allele, the earlier the age of onset of symptoms.

The mutant huntingtin is selective in terms of the damage it causes. Most of the damage occurs to medium-size spiny neurons, nerve cells that form something of a switchboard connecting cells in different parts of the brain. They form a major part of the basal ganglia of the brain. The basal ganglia itself is a structure in the central part of the brain that filters transmissions of nerve signals between the cerebral cortex and the brain's motor centers, thus playing a key role in initiating and controlling movement. It is composed of three primary structures, the **globus pallidus**, the **putamen,** and the **caudate nucleus**—the latter two are collectively known as the **corpus striatum**—as well as smaller structures, such as the **subthalamic nucleus**. Nerve cells in

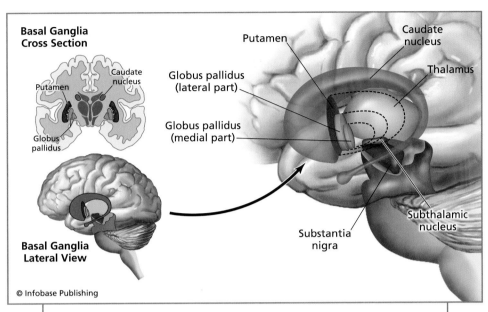

Basal Ganglia
Cross Section

Caudate
nucleus

Putamen

Globus
pallidus

Putamen

Caudate
nucleus

Thalamus

Globus pallidus
(lateral part)

Globus pallidus
(medial part)

Subthalamic
nucleus

Substantia
nigra

Basal Ganglia
Lateral View

© Infobase Publishing

FIGURE 7.3 Damage to cells in the basal ganglia and related structures in the brain is responsible for some of the symptoms of Huntington's disease.

the cerebral cortex are likewise affected. As the damaged neurons shrink and die, the affected parts of the brain atrophy. Brains of persons with severe cases of Huntington's disease weigh as much as 25% less than normal.

While the exact mechanism of nerve cell destruction is not yet known, mutant huntingtin may trigger increased nerve cell mortality because of inappropriate activation of apoptosis; increased excitotoxicity, which may be increased by formation of free radicals; highly reactive compounds; or impaired mitochondrial function. The **mitochondria** are the powerhouses of the cell, producing energy by cellular respiration—a process that releases energy stored in glucose, the only fuel that nerve cells can use. It is analogous to producing heat and light by burning wood on a fire, but in this case the sugar is broken down into carbon dioxide and water (as much of the wood is in a fire), and the energy released is stored in a molecule called adenosine triphosphate, or ATP, which transports the stored energy to wherever it is needed inside the cell. Mutant huntingtin, or fragments of it, can clump together in the nucleus of affected cells, but whether these clumps cause harm or protect the cells by keeping the mutant protein out of the way and out of trouble is not yet known.

Early on, most of the nerve destruction occurs in the globus pallidus, which, because of its role in the regulation of movement—particularly in conjunction with the subthalamic nucleus—may explain the appearance of chorea that gave the disease its initial name. The damage spreads to the corpus striatum, leading to rigidity and **dystonia**—sustained muscle contractions leading to repetitive and twisting movements or abnormal postures. Eventually, other parts of the brain, such as the cerebral cortex and cerebellum, are affected, leading to other symptoms of the disease, such as behavioral disturbances, cognitive declines, and so on. Not all nerve cells are equally affected. Effects of mutant huntingtin vary by nerve cell type, location, and neurotransmitters carried by the cell. **Gliosis**, the formation of scar tissue by an accumulation of **astrocytes**—support cells involved in nervous system repair—indicates nerve cell damage and death.

Given the many potential ways that mutant huntingtin may trigger the nervous system damage seen in Huntington's disease, researchers have had a difficult time devising a cure. But there have been advances in the development of treatments that can delay the onset of symptoms or that can mute the symptoms once they appear.

SEARCH FOR A CURE

A **woman in her mid-40s has been clumsier than usual.**
She has also been a bit more emotionally volatile than
normal and more forgetful, but the constant bruises from
running into the furniture are what really has her worried.
She goes to the doctor, who asks a lot of questions—especially about family medical history—but nothing in her
answers provides a clue. She has no family history of Huntington's disease.

Over time, the symptoms worsen. The doctor decides
it is time for a more rigorous physical examination and
notices, among other things, that the woman's **saccadic
eye movements**—rapid, coordinated eye movements as
the brain rapidly takes in the details of a scene—are slower
than normal. While her eyes have a full range of motion,
their movements in tracking a moving object are jerky. Her
eyebrows twitch, and her tongue tends to move in a subtle
but rapid and involuntary fashion. A potentially serious neurological problem is indicated.

The woman is sent to a radiologist, who, after high-
resolution magnetic resolution imaging (MRI) analysis,
reports atrophy is indicated in several areas of her brain.
Her physician then suggests a genetic test for the Huntington's disease allele.

She tests positive. Her parents are then tested, and her father, while not having the disease himself, has 34 CAG repeats in the polyglutamine region of his IT15 gene. The doctor suspects that a **germ-line mutation** in the father allowed him to pass the disease to the daughter.

As the diagnosis sinks in, the woman asks, "What can be done?"

DELAYING ACTIONS

Despite the fact that the mutation causing the disease has been known for more than 15 years, and that the gene for huntingtin has been completely sequenced, there is as yet no cure for Huntington's disease. (Unlike infectious diseases, there are few cures for genetic diseases.) The most realistic hope at present is to find a way to delay or prevent the progression of the disease so that it becomes a chronic disease, such as asthma, rather than the deadly disease it has been through most of its history.

For most of the century since George Huntington's classic paper was published, the focus on the treatment of Huntington's disease was on managing symptoms—in particular the movement and psychological disturbances that accompany the disease. Drugs such as haloperidol, clozapine, and aripiprazole (often used to treat schizophrenia and other psychoses) or clonazepam (used as a muscle relaxer as well as to prevent convulsions) help control choreic movements; they are also useful in controlling some of the psychotic effects of the disease such as hallucinations and violent outbursts. Unfortunately, such drugs may worsen another muscular effect of the disease—dystonia.

In August 1998, the U.S. Food and Drug Administration (FDA) approved tetrabenazine—a drug known since the 1950s and used in other countries to treat hyperkinetic disorders (uncontrolled muscle movement disorders)—for the treatment of chorea in Huntington's disease patients. It was the first drug in the United States to be specifically approved for such use. Tetrabenazine decreases the amount of dopamine, a neurotransmitter implicated in a number of movement disorders such as Parkinson's disease, available to some nerve cells. By doing so, it inhibits signal transmission between the two and helps control involuntary movements associated with Huntington's and related diseases.

Huntington's disease patients are prone to depression, and some, such as Phebe Hedges, commit suicide. Common antidepressant drugs such as fluoxetine, sertraline, and nortriptyline are used to manage depression in Huntington's patients as well. Lithium, long used to treat **bipolar disorder** (manic depression), can likewise be used to control the volatile mood swings in Huntington's disease as well. Tranquilizers may also be used to control anxiety.

Developing new treatments to prevent or delay the neurological damage that results from the disease, however, has proved to be a significant challenge for Huntington's disease researchers. First, not enough is known about the function of either the wild-type or mutant huntingtin protein. But advances have been made based on what is known today. Current drug development strategies focus on either counteracting the adverse effects of mutant huntingtin or enhancing the functions of wild-type huntingtin.

One of the effects of mutant huntingtin is aggregation (clumping) of the misshapen protein. The aggregates appear to be targeted for destruction and clearing by the cell, but as the aggregates overwhelm the cell's capacity to do so, they build up. While some researchers argue that the clumping has a protective effect, more argue that the clumps are evidence of harm to the cell. Various experiments have shown that a number of drugs that inhibit clumping likewise reduce toxic effects. Benzothiazoles, Congo red (a dye), and trehalose have shown promise in preventing aggregates from forming in experimental systems, as have antibodies that bind to the polyproline segment of the huntingtin gene.

CARING FOR HUNTINGTON'S PATIENTS

While drug therapy is important for slowing—or potentially reversing—the neurological damage associated with Huntington's disease, such treatment is just a subset of the care that persons with the disease require. Proper care involves a multidisciplinary team—which includes physicians and nurses, of course, but also psychologists, social workers, and dieticians, in addition to physical, occupational, and speech and language therapists.

In the early stage of the disease, counseling is especially important in helping the patient as well as family members adjust to the diagnosis and prepare for the changes that will inevitably come. For example, behavioral changes may affect the patient's ability to function at work; slowed reaction time may affect the patient's ability to drive. As economic and other responsibilities within the family shift, significant strains are placed on the family. Without adequate support, some families may disintegrate after one of the members becomes more and more impaired in his or her daily lives.

In the middle stage of the disease, movement disorders become more prominent. Physical and occupational therapy becomes more important, in part to help the patient learn to adjust to the increasing physical disability, but also to help modify the living and working environment so that it becomes less of a hazard to someone afflicted with Huntington's disease. Exercise programs may improve mobility. As speech may be

Caspases are enzymes that break down proteins, or aggregations of proteins such as those formed by mutant huntingtin, inside the cell. Caspase activation plays a role in triggering apoptosis; therefore, research has been devoted to finding ways to minimize death of neurons by inhibiting

affected, speech therapy helps a Huntington's patient prolong the time he or she can communicate with others in their lives. At this point, professionals may be called upon to help plan for the end of the patient's life; a lawyer especially might be required to draw up an advanced directive or a will. Family members might need to be trained in techniques to prolong the patient's life, such as feeding methods, among other things.

By the late stage of the disease, the patient is likely to be institutionalized. Whether or not the patient is in an institution, the focus is on making final preparations for the end of the patient's life and on **palliative care** to minimize the patient's discomfort. Changes often need to be made at home—such as padding the area around the bed—so that the patient does not get hurt by hitting something during uncontrollable, choreic movements. Care of the mouth and patience during feeding are very important, for as the disease nears its end, the patient may be unable to get enough nutrition. Loss of muscular control may prevent a Huntington's patient from closing his or her mouth properly (and keeping the food in), chewing it properly, or even swallowing it without difficulty. Feeding through a tube is typically needed in the end stages, although patients in some cases may refuse such life-support measures—if they are deemed legally competent to make such decisions at the time, or if they have made their wishes for end-of-life care known in advance.

caspase activity. An antibiotic, minocycline, has recently shown promise in blocking caspase activation, as well as protecting nerve cells in other ways. A bile acid, taurourso-deoxycholic acid, has been tested in animal studies, where it has demonstrated promise in reducing apoptosis, as well as reducing atrophy and leading to fewer and smaller aggregations of mutant huntingtin.

Mutant huntingtin increases neuron vulnerability to exci-totoxicity in several ways. First, it may make a nerve cell vulnerable to chemicals that alter the activity of glutamate—an excitatory neurotransmitter derived from glutamine—receptors on the cell membrane. It may also lead to elevated neurotransmitter levels by altering the transport of the chemicals both within the cell and outside of the cell across the cell membrane at the synapse. The overly sensitive and overworked cell receiving the chemical signal dies from the resulting overexposure to glutamate. The glutamate triggers an influx of ions—particularly calcium—into the cell, which activates a number of enzymes that damage cell structures. Several experiments have been conducted focusing on drugs that block either the release of glutamate or the activity of N-methyl-D-aspartate (NMDA) receptors. So far, no good candidates for drug therapies have emerged from that research. Maintaining a normal level of receptor activity while inhibiting excess activity—and while minimizing side effects—has been and remains a challenge.

A number of investigators have found evidence of mito-chondrial dysfunction in patients with Huntington's disease. Defects in the energy production system damage cells through the accumulation of free radicals—highly reactive molecules that, by reacting with other molecules, inhibit or destroy the function of those other molecules. The oxygen molecule itself, while not a free radical, is also highly reactive. Buildup of oxygen levels inside the cell can likewise inhibit or destroy the function of cell structures. (For example, oxygen, by reacting with iron, causes rust, which weakens and damages materials made of iron or steel.) Antioxidants, such as ascorbate (vitamin C), and compounds that boost ATP production within cells, such as creatine, have been tested for their ability to minimize or reverse nerve cell damage. While some of the compounds tested appear to be more effective in preventing symptoms before they appear, creatine has shown some potential to slow or stop the progression of some effects. Coenzyme Q10 and a related compound, idebenone, function as both antioxidants and energy boosters and have likewise shown potential to slow progression of the disease.

Mutant huntingtin may alter expression of some genes by its interactions with compounds that regulate the transcription of those genes (transcription factors). One method of gene regulation is histone acetylation, in which acetyl groups—a chemical group similar in structure to acetic acid (vinegar)—bind to the histone proteins that help form the structure of chromosomes. Acetylation loosens up the packing around the DNA, exposing genes and making it easier for them to be transcribed. Histone deacetylation leads to increased packing and decreased access to the DNA, which in turn leads to decreased gene activity. Mutant huntingtin appears to reduce levels of acetylated histones in cell cultures. Some researchers are investigating whether compounds that inhibit histone deacetylation may likewise reduce neuron damage and loss associated with Huntington's disease. Two such inhibitors, valproic acid and sodium phenylbutyrate, are already approved for the treatment of other disorders by the FDA and are now being evaluated for their effectiveness in patients with Huntington's disease.

Another strategy that has shown promise in the treatment of Huntington's and other genetic diseases is in

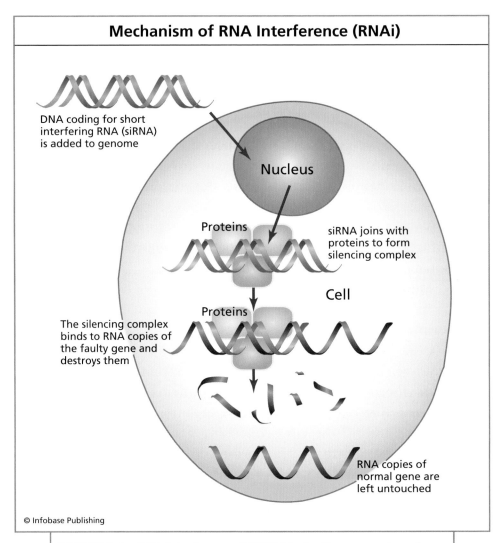

Mechanism of RNA Interference (RNAi)

DNA coding for short interfering RNA (siRNA) is added to genome

Nucleus

Proteins

siRNA joins with proteins to form silencing complex

Cell

Proteins

The silencing complex binds to RNA copies of the faulty gene and destroys them

RNA copies of normal gene are left untouched

© Infobase Publishing

FIGURE 8.1 RNA interference (RNAi) blocks the expression of mutant genes by silencing, or preventing the translation of, RNA copies of the mutant gene.

preventing the expression of alleles that trigger those diseases. Given that most people with Huntington's disease are heterozygous—they have inherited only one copy of the disease-causing allele—it may be possible to prevent the translation (synthesis) of the mutant huntingtin. One way to do so is called RNA interference (RNAi). In RNA interference, special RNA molecules that recognize specific complementary sequences on mRNA can selectively target and either inactivate or destroy mRNA before it can be translated into protein. In research led by Beverly L. Davidson, RNA interference has shown promise in reducing and possibly reversing some of the Huntington's disease–related damage in animal models. In Davidson's work, both the wild-type and mutant huntingtin are targeted. Ideally, such an approach would target only the mutant protein. An effort is now underway to develop a commercially available treatment based on Davidson's research.

THE CRITICAL QUESTION

While there is a genetic test for the Huntington's disease allele, there is as yet no cure. Persons with a family history of the disease face a tremendous dilemma—whether or not to get tested before symptoms develop.

TO TEST OR NOT TO TEST?

When the G8 marker for Huntington's disease was discovered, it paved the way for a genetic test for the disease before symptoms appear—a goal fully realized in 1993 when the gene that codes for the huntingtin protein, IT15, was identified and mapped.

Generally, only persons with a family history of the disease need consider presymptomatic testing. A person who has one parent with the disease usually has a 50% chance of inheriting the mutant allele, although if the parent is homozygous for the mutant allele—has two copies of the allele—there is little need for testing since only a genetic accident prior to or during sperm or egg cell formation will prevent the mutation from being passed on. Confirmatory testing may also be administered to a person with symptoms of the disease, whether that person has a family history of Huntington's, or—as in the example in the previous chapter—the person has no family history of the disease.

The technical part of the test is rather simple: Blood or some other tissue (such as amniotic fluid taken during prenatal testing) is sampled, and the IT15 gene is analyzed for the number of CAG repeats in the polyglutamine segment of the gene. The American College of Medical Genetics/American Society of Human Genetics Huntington Disease

Genetic Testing Working Group issued the following diagnostic guidelines in 1998:

Repeat Length	Disease Risk
< 27	Normal
27–35	Intermediate
36–39	Reduced penetrance
> 39	Full penetrance

A person in the "Normal" category has no risk of developing the disease. Someone in the "Full penetrance" category will develop the disease. Individuals in the "Intermediate" category will not develop the disease, but they are at risk of germ-line expansion mutations that will enable them to pass the disease on to their children (men are especially at risk). Finally, those in the "Reduced penetrance" category may or may not develop the disease. Like those in the "Intermediate" category, however, they are at risk of expansion mutations that could place their children at risk.

While this is relatively straightforward, the actual testing procedure is usually much more involved, given the implications of a positive diagnosis. According to guidelines issued by the Huntington's Disease Society of America (HDSA), substantial pretest and posttest counseling should accompany all clinical work. The HDSA recommends (1) a prescreening interview, whether in person or over the telephone; (2) three pretest, in-person appointments for the purposes of genetic counseling and neurological and psychological evaluation; (3) a fourth in-person appointment for reporting of genetic testing results; and (4) posttest counseling.

Furthermore, the HDSA recommends that persons being tested should be accompanied by someone other than a sibling to all in-person appointments (some researchers suggest that siblings may become upset if one sibling's tests show high risk for Huntington's and another sibling's tests do not—bringing a non-sibling friend to appointments prevents the possibility of guilty or hurt feelings if there is a difference in two siblings' test results); that at least one month should elapse between the final preclinical appointment and the administration of the test (except in the case of prenatal testing); that no one under the age of 18 should be tested unless they are already showing symptoms of the disease; that test results only be given to the person

GENETIC COUNSELING

Why all the pre- and posttest counseling? The answer is simple: A positive test result can be psychologically and emotionally devastating, given the fact that as yet there is no cure—so devastating, in fact, that when the first genetic marker for the disease was discovered, some medical ethicists questioned whether or not it was ethical to tell someone they had a disease that is both deadly and—at least early on—untreatable. For example, a person who learned he had the disease in his twenties could face decades of stress and uncertainty while waiting for the inevitable onset of symptoms and premature death. In general, feelings of depression and hopelessness are heightened for those who test positive than for those who test negative in the initial weeks after receiving the results. The differences between the two groups may or may not diminish over time, but suicide rates are higher in those who carry the Huntington's disease allele (although it is unclear whether such suicides are a consequence of the pathology of the disease or of emotional distress from knowing one will get it). In most cases, those being tested (unless consent has otherwise been granted), and that those results be given in person; and that couples considering prenatal testing should consider testing before conception.

SOCIAL STIGMA

Historically, individuals with Huntington's disease were stigmatized in many communities—even if they were not deemed witches and condemned to being burned at the stake. Other families would, and possibly still do in some

who test positive for the mutant allele adjust to the fact that they will eventually get the disease, but during significant life changes, such as falling in love or having a child, feelings of fear and hopelessness may increase; long-forgotten memories of a parent or relative with the disease may resurface and cause the person to reexperience past trauma.

The stress can take a toll on family and friends of those who carry the Huntington's disease allele. In particular, partners of those who test positive may feel more stressed or pessimistic in the short run. Concerns over children the partners have, or over decisions to have or not have children in the future, may likewise prove stressful. Facing the potential burden of caring for a partner with Huntington's disease may undermine the relationship. Children of those who test positive may be more prone to behavioral problems; in addition, as the affected parent's disease progresses, the parent's behavioral and emotional volatility, in combination with the typical behavioral and emotional volatility of adolescence, may create a rather tense environment at home.

areas, discourage their children from dating or marrying children from families with a history of the disease.

Such taboos made it into law. During the first half of the twentieth century, the United States pioneered the practice of **forced sterilization** in its zeal for **eugenics**, a pseudoscience that advocated the improvement of society by controlling the reproductive decisions of the populace. The first state to pass forced sterilization laws was Indiana in 1907. At one time, as many as 33 states (out of 48 at the time) enforced compulsory sterilization laws intended to rid society of undesirable elements such as criminals, deviants, and the "feeble-minded." Those with Huntington's disease most certainly were caught up in the drive to "improve" American society. Tens of thousands of people were sterilized against their will. The worst aspect of the laws was that children of "undesirables" also could be forcibly sterilized.

REASONS FOR TESTING

Despite the concerns and arguable futility of getting tested for Huntington's disease before symptoms appear, there are reasons to do so. Some individuals find the knowledge that they will get the disease less stressful than the uncertainty. Advanced warning can empower someone to find ways to protect one's health for as long as possible so that the years before symptoms appear can be spent living as full a life as possible—enjoying life while young rather than deferring until a leisurely retirement that will likely never come. Such forewarning may enable someone to take advantage of a novel treatment that, if started early enough, will allow an individual to live a long, relatively happy life denied to his or her ancestors.

In addition, knowing whether or not they will get the disease allows those at risk of developing the disease to make

FORCED STERILIZATION

An unfortunately common attitude toward victims of these laws was shockingly expressed by Supreme Court Justice Oliver Wendell Holmes, who wrote the prevailing opinion in *Buck v. Bell*, a decision that upheld Virginia's desire to forcibly sterilize Carrie Buck, a teenager and single parent, whose mother had a history of "immorality." Holmes wrote:

> The judgment finds the facts that have been recited and that Carrie Buck "is the probable potential parent of socially inadequate offspring, likewise afflicted, that she may be sexually sterilized without detriment to her general health and that her welfare and that of society will

(continues)

In 1927, the courts ruled in the case of *Buck v. Bell* that Carrie Buck (*left*) be sterilized to prevent further generations of people considered "imbeciles." Her mother (*right*) was also thought to be mentally disabled and therefore considered a threat to society.

(continued)

be promoted by her sterilization," and thereupon makes the order. . . . We have seen more than once that the public welfare may call upon the best citizens for their lives. It would be strange if it could not call upon those who already sap the strength of the State for these lesser sacrifices, often not felt to be such by those concerned, in order to prevent our being swamped with incompetence. *It is better for all the world, if instead of waiting to execute degenerate offspring for crime, or to let them starve for their imbecility, society can prevent those who are manifestly unfit from continuing their kind. The principle that sustains compulsory vaccination is broad enough to cover cutting the Fallopian tubes. . . . Three generations of imbeciles are enough.*[21] [emphasis added]

Adolf Hitler and his Third Reich learned quite a bit about social "improvement" from the United States—to the extent of vigorous scientific cooperation between U.S. and German scientists in the early years of Hitler's regime. Those with Huntington's disease were specifically targeted by Germany's sterilization law, which was enacted in 1933. Hundreds of thousands of people were ordered to be forcibly sterilized by German eugenics courts by the time the Nazi regime was destroyed at the end of World War II.

Today, those at risk of Huntington's disease do not have to worry about forced sterilization. However, information about their genetic legacy can be misused—they may be denied or dismissed from jobs, denied insurance benefits, or shunned by their neighbors if the results of a test for Huntington's disease fall into the wrong hands.

an informed decision about whether or not to have children. Some know they will eventually get Huntington's disease and decide to have children anyway. Others decide not to. Some parents at risk of the disease use prenatal testing to determine whether or not to terminate a pregnancy if the fetus has the mutant allele. Others use prenatal testing and have the child anyway. In the end, such decisions can be made solely by the person and his or her partner.

REASON FOR HOPE

In the early 1980s, testing positive for the human immunodeficiency virus (HIV) was regarded as a death sentence from acquired immune deficiency syndrome (AIDS) within a relatively short time. People at risk often avoided getting tested for the virus because they feared the consequence of the knowledge—a death preceded by a dramatic and sometimes agonizing decline, much like a diagnosis of Huntington's disease has been. In the years since, however, a number of therapies have been developed that allow those with HIV/AIDS to live long, productive, and happy lives. There is still no cure, but the symptoms can be managed and the progression of the disease held in check.

In many ways, the improved understanding of Huntington's disease has set the foundation for a similar revolution. A number of potential therapies have been developed that one day may allow Huntington's disease patients to live longer, more productive, and happier lives after initial symptoms appear. Researchers around the world are racing to find ways to bring the revolution about. Dozens of new research papers on the topic appear every month, and there is little sign that the scientific activity will slow down. It is a fascinating time, both for those affected by the disease as well as those merely interested in it.

NOTES

1. Ed Cray, *Ramblin' Man: The Life and Times of Woody Guthrie* (New York: W.W. Norton, 2004), 33.

2. Joe Klein, *Woody Guthrie: A Life* (New York: Dell, 1999), 49.

3. Cray, *Ramblin' Man*, 352.

4. Cray, *Ramblin' Man*, 352.

5. J.F.C. Hecker, *The Epidemics of the Middle Ages*, 3rd ed., trans. B.G. Babington (London: Trübner & Company, 1859), 80.

6. Hecker, *Epidemics of the Middle Ages*, 92.

7. Thomas Sydenham, *The Works of Thomas Sydenham, M.D.*, translated from the Latin edition of Dr. Greenhill with a Life of the Author by Robert Gordon Latham. (London: Sydenham Society, 1850), 257–258.

8. John Elliotson, "St. Thomas's Hospital. Clinical Lecture," *Lancet* 1 (1832): 163.

9. Douglas J. Lanska, "George Huntington (1850–1916) and Hereditary Chorea," *Journal of the History of the Neurosciences* 9 (2000): 79.

10. Lanska, "George Huntington," 80.

11. Alf L. Ørbeck, "An Early Description of Huntington's Chorea," *Medical History* 3 (1959): 165.

12. George Huntington, "Recollections of Huntington's Chorea as I Saw It at East Hampton, Long Island, During my Boyhood," *Journal of Nervous and Mental Diseases* 37 (1910): 255–256.

13. George Huntington, "On Chorea," *Medical and Surgical Reporter: A Weekly Journal* 26 (1872): 320–321.

14. William Osler, "Historical Note on Hereditary Chorea," *Neurographs* 1 (1908): 115.

15. August Weismann, *The Germ-Plasm: A Theory of Heredity*, trans. W. Newton Parker and Harriet Rönnefeldt (New York: Charles Scribner's Sons, 1893), 453.

16. "Sag Harbor," *Suffolk Gazette*, June 30, 1806.

17. Kathleen Danna and Daniel Nathans, "Specific Cleavage of Simian Virus 40 DNA by Restriction Endonuclease

of Hemophilus influenzae," *Proceedings of the National Academy of Sciences of the United States of America* 68 (1971): 2917.

18. Michael S. Okun and Nia Thommi, "Americo Negrette (1924 to 2003): Diagnosing Huntington Disease in Venezuela," *Neurology* 63 (2004): 341.

19. Okun and Thommi, "Americo Negrette," 341.

20. Okun and Thommi, "Americo Negrette," 341.

21. *Buck v. Bell*, 274 United States Supreme Court Reports 200 (1927).

GLOSSARY

Alleles   Alternate versions of genes; alleles are responsible for the variation in genetic traits, such as flower color in the pea (*Pisum sativum*).

Amino acid   A type of molecule that serves as the basic building block of proteins (polypeptides).

Androgen   A steroid compound that acts as a male sex hormone.

Anticodon   A three-nucleotide sequence on transfer RNA (tRNA) that recognizes a complementary codon on messenger RNA; in protein synthesis, the complementary pairing of anticodons and codons ensures that the resulting protein contains the proper amino acid sequence.

Apoptosis   Programmed cell death in response to stimuli that activates what is essentially a cell suicide pathway.

Astrocytes   Cells that provide metabolic and structural support for nerve cells.

Ataxia   A loss of muscle coordination during movement.

Autoradiograph   A type of X-ray image that uses radiation emitted by the object of interest to expose a film or digital sensor.

Autosome   A non-sex chromosome; in other words, a chromosome not involved in determining the sex of an individual.

Avirulent   Not capable of causing disease.

Bacteriophage (also phage)   A virus that infects bacteria.

Bipolar disorder (or manic depression) A mental disorder characterized by extreme mood swings alternating between states of depression and mania.

Brain-derived neurotrophic factor (BDNF) A protein that promotes the growth, development, health, and survival of brain cells.

Caspase An enzyme that breaks down proteins and clumps of proteins.

Caudate nucleus One of the three paired basal ganglia (which include the globus pallidus and putamen), containing nerve cells that, by acting as a switchboard in the brain, are involved in regulating movement, cognitive activity, emotions, and memory in the brain.

Centrifugation A method of separating molecular or cellular components by rapidly spinning suspensions of the components for a selected period of time.

Chorea A neurological disorder characterized by movements that mimic normal, voluntary actions, but that instead occur randomly, sometimes wildly, without coordination or individual control.

Chromatin A complex of deoxyribonucleic acid (DNA) and protein that makes up chromosomes.

Chromosome A structure made of chromatin that contains genes.

Codon A three-nucleotide sequence on messenger RNA (mRNA) that, during protein synthesis, either codes for a specific amino acid or signals the end of a newly made polypeptide chain.

Cognitive Involving knowledge, perception, memory, and judgment.

Corpus striatum A structure in the brain's basal ganglia made of the caudate nucleus and putamen.

Dalton A unit used to measure atomic or molecular weight that is about equal to the mass of one proton or neutron.

Dance of St. John A type of dancing mania in the Middle Ages characterized by wild, uncontrollable, and sometimes violent behavior.

Denature To make a molecule lose its ability to function by altering its structure.

Deoxyribonucleic acid (DNA) The molecule that carries genetic information in the sequence of nucleotide bases along the length of the paired strands that comprise its double-helix structure.

Deoxyribose A five-carbon sugar that is a key component of the structure of DNA.

Dominant A genetic trait that is always expressed when the allele that codes for it is present.

Dystonia A disorder characterized by sustained muscle contractions leading to repetitive, twisting movements or abnormal postures.

Endonuclease An enzyme that breaks down nucleic acids by splitting bonds between the nucleotides within the chain (as opposed to exonucleases, which trim nucleic acids one at a time from the ends of the chain).

Enzyme A protein that catalyzes (initiates or speeds up) chemical reactions.

Eugenics A pseudoscience that advocates "improvement" of the human race by limiting reproduction of "unde-sirables" and/or promoting reproduction of favored individuals.

Excitotoxicity A type of nerve cell toxicity triggered by excess stimulation (excitement) of nerve cells by the neurotransmitter glutamate.

Exon A portion of a gene that codes for either protein or functional RNA such as ribosomal RNA (rRNA) or transfer RNA (tRNA).

Exon amplification A method of isolating a DNA fragment, such as a gene, of interest by making copies of it using some kind of cellular host.

Expansion mutation A mutation that lengthens, or expands, a gene by repeatedly duplicating nucleotide sequences on a chromosome.

Forced sterilization Making an unwilling person sterile (unable to have children) by forcing them to undergo some kind of medical procedure that results in sterility. Used as a tool to "improve" races by advocates of eugenics.

Gel electrophoresis A method of separating proteins or nucleic acids on the basis of size and electrical charge.

Gene The basic unit of inheritance; a segment of DNA that contains the code for a specific inherited trait.

Genome The full complement of genes in an individual.

Genomic imprinting Modification of how an allele is expressed depending on whether it is inherited from the female or male parent.

Germ cells Egg or sperm cells, that is, sex cells. In sexually reproducing organisms, an egg and sperm cell fuse to form a new individual.

Germ-line mutation A mutation in a cell that gives rise to germ cells.

Gliosis An accumulation of astrocytes in damaged areas of the brain that leads to the formation of scar tissue.

Globus pallidus   One of the three paired basal ganglia (which include the caudate nucleus and putamen) containing nerve cells that, by acting as a switchboard and filter in the brain, are involved in regulating movement.

Heterozygous   A condition that occurs when an individual has two different alleles for a given gene.

Homologous pair   Two chromosomes that contain the same set of genes.

Homozygous   A condition that occurs when an individual has two copies of the same allele for a given gene.

Incomplete dominance   A phenomenon by which the characteristic of a heterozygous individual is intermediate between the characteristics of the two parental alleles. An example would be a red-flowered snapdragon crossed with a white-flowered one; the resulting offspring would have pink flowers.

Intron   A portion of a gene that does not code for any kind of functional product, whether protein or functional RNA.

Karyotype   An image of the full complement of chromosomes in an individual in which the chromosomes are ordered in homologous pairs sorted from the longest pair of autosomes to the shortest pair of autosomes, followed by the sex chromosomes

Linked genes   Genes located on the same chromosome.

Meiosis   The two-division process that produces germ cells in sexually reproducing organisms. It begins with a precursor cell that has two copies of each chromosome; after the second division, there are four daughter cells that each has one copy of each chromosome.

Messenger RNA (mRNA)   A type of RNA made as a copy of a gene that serves as the blueprint for the assembly of polypeptides by ribosomes.

Mitochondria   The organelle, or structure, in a cell that produces energy by cellular respiration; essentially a chemical combustion of a sugar fuel.

Mitosis   A division of a cell that produces two daughter cells that are genetically identical to the parent cell.

Mutation   A change in nucleotide sequence that may alter the product coded for by a gene.

Myopathy   A disease or abnormality of muscle tissue.

Neurodegenerative disease   A disorder or disease characterized by damage to and degeneration of nervous tissue.

Nitrogenous base   An organic base containing nitrogen. Several nitrogenous bases are key components of nucleic acids. DNA has adenine, guanine, cytosine, and thymine; RNA has adenine, guanine, and cytosine, but has uracil instead of thymine.

Nucleotide   A type of molecule that serves as the basic building block of nucleic acids; nucleotides consist of three components: a five-carbon sugar, a phosphate group, and a nitrogenous base.

Palliative care   Care devoted to making a patient as comfortable as possible by reducing the severity of the symptoms of a disease; it is usually the focus in severe cases when a cure is unlikely or impossible.

Penetrance   A measure of the likelihood that an individual carrying a specific allele will develop the trait coded for by that allele.

Phage (see bacteriophage)

Plasmid   A DNA molecule that is not part of a chromosome. Plasmids, which are typically circular, are common in bacteria and yeasts and can be exchanged between cells as well as used to introduce novel genes into cells.

Polypeptide (see protein)

Polysaccharides A molecule made of repeating units called sugars.

Prevalence The total number of people with a given illness.

Protein (also polypeptide) A molecule made of repeating units called amino acids.

Putamen One of the three paired basal ganglia (which include the caudate nucleus and globus pallidus), containing nerve cells that, by acting as a switchboard and filter in the brain, are involved in regulating movement.

Recessive An allele whose trait is only expressed if the individual is homozygous (has two copies of the allele).

Restriction enzyme An enzyme that cuts nucleic acids at specific nucleotide sequences.

Restriction fragment Fragment of DNA or RNA created by allowing restriction enzymes to chop up the genome.

Restriction fragment length polymorphism (RFLP) Variation in the length of restriction fragments; the presence of RFLPs indicates genetic differences among the individuals analyzed.

Reverse transcriptase An enzyme that synthesizes DNA from an RNA template.

Rheumatic fever An inflammatory disease cause by infection by Group A Streptococcus bacteria.

Ribonucleic acid (RNA) A nucleic acid that serves a variety of functions inside a cell. Similar to DNA in basic structure, RNA may be the sole medium for the storage of genetic information in some viruses.

Ribosomal RNA (rRNA) A specialized type of RNA that forms structural components of ribosomes.

Ribosome The organelle (structure in a cell) responsible for making polypeptides based on blueprint information contained in mRNA.

Saccadic eye movements Rapid, coordinated eye movements as the brain rapidly scans and takes in the details of a scene.

St. Vitus's dance In medieval times, a name for a type of dancing mania; more recently, the term has been used to refer to the diseases now known as Sydenham's chorea and Huntington's disease. Today, the term is used primarily for Sydenham's chorea.

Scintillation counter An instrument used to detect and measure radiation levels in a sample.

Sex chromosome A chromosome involved in determining the sex of an individual.

Sex-linked trait A trait whose gene is located on one of the sex chromosomes.

Somatic cell Any cell in a multicellular organism other than eggs or sperm.

Somatic cell hybrid A hybrid created by fusing somatic cells of two different species.

Stop codon A codon that signals the end of a polypeptide chain.

Subthalamic nucleus A paired concentration of nerve cells in the brain that, by integrating with the basal ganglia and midbrain, is involved in regulating movement.

Synapsis The pairing up of homologous chromosomes during an early stage of meiosis.

Transcription The process by which messenger RNA is assembled based on a template encoded in a gene.

Transfer RNA (tRNA) A specialized type of RNA responsible for recognizing a specific amino acid and bringing it to a ribosome, where it can be assembled into a polypeptide chain.

Translation The process by which ribosomes assemble polypeptides based on a template encoded in messenger RNA.

Trinucleotide A three-nucleotide sequence in a nucleic acid.

Trinucleotide repeat A trinucleotide sequence repeated over and over in a gene; too many or too few trinucleotide repeats in certain genes may trigger genetic diseases.

Unlinked genes Genes located on different chromosomes.

Virulent Capable of causing disease.

BIBLIOGRAPHY

American College of Medical Genetics/American Society of Human Genetics Huntington Disease Genetic Testing Working Group. "ACMG/ASHG Statement: Laboratory Guidelines for Huntington Disease Genetic Testing." *American Journal of Human Genetics* 62 (1998): 1243–1247.

Arber, Werner. "Host-controlled Modification of Bacteriophage." *Annual Review of Microbiology* 19 (1965): 365–378.

Avery, Oswald T., Collin M. MacLeod, and Maclyn McCarty. "Studies on the Chemical Nature of the Substance Inducing Transformation of Pneumococcal Types: Induction of Transformation by a Deoxyribonucleic Acid Fraction Isolated from Pneumococcus Type III." *Journal of Experimental Medicine* 79 (1944): 137–158.

Aylward, E.H., B.F. Sparks, K.M. Field, V. Yallapragada, B.D. Shpritz, A. Rosenblatt, J. Brandt, et al. "Onset and Rate of Striatal Atrophy in Preclinical Huntington Disease." *Neurology* 63 (2004): 66–72.

Bates, Gillian. "Huntingtin Aggregation and Toxicity in Huntington's Disease." *Lancet* 361 (2003): 1642–1644.

Bates, G.P., M.E. MacDonald, S. Baxendale, S. Youngman, C. Lin, W.L. Whaley, J.J. Wasmuth, et al. "Defined Physical Limits of the Huntington Disease Gene Candidate Region." *American Journal of Human Genetics* 49 (1991): 7–16.

Bateson, William. *Mendel's Principles of Heredity: A Defence, with a Translation of Mendel's Original Papers on Hybridisation.* Cambridge: University Press, 1902.

Bertani, G., and J.J. Weigle. "Host Controlled Variation in Bacterial Viruses." *Journal of Bacteriology* 65 (1953): 113–121.

Black, Edwin. *War Against the Weak: Eugenics and America's Campaign to Create a Master Race.* New York: Thunder's Mouth Press, 2004.

Blekher, Tanya, Marjorie R. Weaver, Jeanine Marshall, Siu Hui, Jacqueline Gray Jackson, Julie C. Stout, Xabier Beristain, et al. "Visual Scanning and Cognitive Performance in Prediagnostic and Early-stage Huntington's Disease." *Movement Disorders* (in press).

Brown, Trevor, and John F. Sander. "Chorea." *American Journal of Nursing* 25 (1925): 921–923.

Browning, William. "Bibliography." *Neurographs* 1 (1908): 153–164.

———. "Dr. Charles Rollin Gorman." *Neurographs* 1 (1908): 144–147.

———. "Irving Whitehall Lyon, M.D." *Neurographs* 1 (1908): 147–149.

———. "Rev. Charles Oscar Waters, M.D." *Neurographs* 1 (1908): 137–144.

Bruinius, Harry. *Better for All the World: The Secret History of Forced Sterilization and America's Quest for Racial Purity.* New York: Alfred A. Knopf, 2006.

Brusa, Livia, Antonio Orlacchio, Vincenzo Moschella, Moschella Cesare, Iani Giorgio, Bernardi Nicola, and Biagio Mercuri. "Treatment of the Symptoms of Huntington's Disease: Preliminary Results Comparing Aripiprazole and Tetrabenazine." *Movement Disorders* (in press).

Buck v. Bell. 274 United States Supreme Court Reports 200 (1927).

Buckler, A.J., D.D. Chang, S.L. Graw, J.D. Brook, D.A. Haber, P.A. Sharp, and D.E. Housman. "Exon Amplification: A Strategy to Isolate Mammalian Genes Based on RNA Splicing."

Proceedings of the National Academy of Sciences of the United States of America 88 (1991): 4005–4009.

Campbell, Neil A., Jane B. Reece, Lisa A. Urry, Michael L. Cain, Steven A. Wasserman, Peter V. Minorsky, and Robert B. Jackson. *Biology*, 8th ed. San Francisco: Pearson Benjamin Cummings, 2008.

Cattaneo, Elena, Chiara Zuccato, and Marzia Tartari. "Normal Huntingtin Function: An Alternative Approach to Huntington's Disease." *Nature Reviews Neuroscience* 6 (2005): 919–930.

Conneally, P.M. "Huntington's Disease: Genetics and Epidemiology." *American Journal of Human Genetics* 36 (1984): 506–526.

Cray, Ed. *Ramblin' Man: The Life and Times of Woody Guthrie.* New York: W.W. Norton, 2004.

Crick, F.H.C. "Ideas on Protein Synthesis." Unpublished notes, 1956.

———. "On Protein Synthesis." *Symposia of the Society for Experimental Biology* 12 (1958): 138–163.

———. "Central Dogma of Molecular Biology." *Nature* 227 (1970): 561–563.

Danna, Kathleen, and Daniel Nathans. "Specific Cleavage of Simian Virus 40 DNA by Restriction Endonuclease of *Hemophilus influenzae.*" *Proceedings of the National Academy of Sciences of the United States of America* 68 (1971): 2913–2917.

Di Prospero, Nicholas A., and Kenneth H. Fischbeck. "Therapeutics Development for Triplet Repeat Expansion Diseases." *Nature Reviews Genetics* 6 (2005): 756–767.

Duisterhof, Magdalena, Rutger W. Trijsburg, Martinus F. Niermeijer, Raymund A.C. Roos, and Aad Tibben. "Psychological Studies in Huntington's Disease: Making up the Balance." *Journal of Medical Genetics* 38 (2001): 852–861.

Elliotson, John. "St. Thomas's Hospital. Clinical Lecture." *Lancet* 1 (1832): 161–167.

Food and Drug Administration. *FDA Approves First Drug for Treatment of Chorea in Huntington's Disease.* Rockville, Md.: Food and Drug Administration, 2008. Available online. URL: http://www.fda.gov/bbs/topics/NEWS/2008/NEW01874. html.

Franklin, R.E., and R.G. Gosling. "Molecular Configuration in Sodium Thymonucleate." *Nature* 171 (1953): 740–741.

Goetz, Christopher G., Theresa A. Chmura, and Douglas J. Lanska. "History of Chorea: Part 3 of the MDS-sponsored History of Movement Disorders Exhibit, Barcelona, June 2000." *Movement Disorders* 16 (2001): 331–338.

Goldberg, Y. Paul, Cynthia T. McMurray, Jutta Zeisier, Elisabeth Almqvist, David Sillence, Flona Richards, A. Marquis Gacy, et al. "Increased Instability of Intermediate Alleles in Families With Sporadic Huntington Disease Compared to Similar Sized Intermediate Alleles in the General Population." *Human Molecular Genetics* 4 (1995): 1911–1918.

Griffith, Fred. "The Significance of Pneumococcal Types." *Journal of Hygiene* 27 (1928): 113–159.

Grunberg-Manago, Marianne, Priscilla J. Ortiz, and Severo Ochoa. "Enzymatic Synthesis of Nucleic Acidlike Polynucleotides." *Science* 122 (1955): 907–910.

Gusella, James F., Nancy S. Wexler, P. Michael Conneally, Susan L. Naylor, Mary Anne Anderson, Rudolph E. Tanzi, Paul C. Watkins, et al. "A Polymorphic DNA Marker Genetically Linked to Huntington's Disease." *Nature* 306 (1983): 234–238.

Gusella, James F., Rudolph E. Tanzi, Patricia I. Bader, Mary C. Phelan, Roger Stevenson, Michael R. Hayden, Karen J. Hofman, et al. "Deletion of Huntington's Disease–linked G8

(D4S10) Locus in Wolf-Hirschhorn Syndrome." *Nature* 318 (1985): 75–78.

Harper, Peter S. "The Epidemiology of Huntington's Disease." *Human Genetics* 89 (1992): 365–376.

Harper, Scott Q., Patrick D. Staber, Xiaohua He, Steven L. Eliason, Inês H. Martins, Qinwen Mao, Linda Yang, et al. "RNA Interference Improves Motor and Neuropathological Abnormalities in a Huntington's Disease Mouse Model." *Proceedings of the National Academy of Sciences of the United States of America* 102 (2005): 5820–5825.

Hecker, J.F.C. *The Epidemics of the Middle Ages*, 3rd ed. Trans. B.G. Babington. London: Trübner & Company, 1859.

Henig, Robin Marantz. *The Monk in the Garden: The Lost and Found Genius of Gregor Mendel, the Father of Genetics*. Boston: Houghton-Mifflin, 2000.

Hershey, A.D., and Martha Chase. "Independent Functions of Viral Protein and Nucleic Acid in Growth of Bacteriophage." *Journal of General Physiology* 36 (1952): 39–56.

Huntington, George. "On Chorea." *Medical and Surgical Reporter: A Weekly Journal* 26 (1872): 317–321.

———. "Recollections of Huntington's Chorea as I Saw It at East Hampton, Long Island, During My Boyhood." *Journal of Nervous and Mental Diseases* 37 (1910): 255–257.

Huntington Family Association. *The Huntington Family in America: A Genealogical Memoir of the Known Descendants of Simon Huntington from 1633 to 1915, Including those Who Have Retained the Family Name, and Many Bearing Other Surnames*. Hartford, Conn.: Huntington Family Association, 1915.

The Huntington's Disease Collaborative Research Group. "A Novel Gene Containing a Trinucleotide Repeat That Is Expanded and Unstable on Huntington's Disease Chromosomes." *Cell* 72 (1993): 971–983.

Innes, A.M., and A.E. Chudley. "Genetic Landmarks Through Philately: Woodrow Wilson 'Woody' Guthrie and Huntington disease." *Clinical Genetics* 61 (2002): 263–267.

Kao, Fa-Ten, and Theodore T. Puck. "Genetics of Somatic Mammalian Cells: Linkage Studies with Human-Chinese Hamster Cell Hybrids." *Nature* 228 (1970): 329–332.

Kelly, Thomas J., and Hamilton O. Smith. "A Restriction Enzyme from *Hemophilus influenzae*: II. Base Sequence of the recognition site." *Journal of Molecular Biology* 51 (1970): 393–409.

Kenney, Christopher, Christine Hunter, Anthony Davidson, and Joseph Jankovic. "Short-term Effects of Tetrabenazine on Chorea Associated with Huntington's Disease." *Movement Disorders* 22 (2007): 10–13.

Kieburtz, Karl, Marcy MacDonald, Charles Shih, Andrew Feigin, Kim Steinberg, Kathy Bordwell, Carol Zimmerman, Jayalakshmi Srinidhi, Jenny Sotack, James Gusella, and Ira Shoulson. "Trinucleotide Repeat Length and Progression of Illness in Huntington's Disease." *Journal of Medical Genetics* 31 (1994): 872–874.

Klein, Joe. *Woody Guthrie: A Life.* New York: Dell, 1999.

Kleppe, K., E. Ohtsuka, R. Kleppe, I. Molineux, and H.G. Khorana. "Studies on Polynucleotides: XCVI. Repair replication of short synthetic DNAs as catalyzed by DNA polymerases." *Journal of Molecular Biology* 56 (1971): 341–361.

Krack, Paul. "Relicts of Dancing Mania: The Dancing Procession of Echternach." *Neurology* 53 (1999): 2169–2172.

Kremer, Berry, Paul Goldberg, Susan E. Andrew, Jane Theilmann, Hakan Telenius, Jutta Zeisler, Ferdinando Squitieri, et al. "A Worldwide Study of the Huntington's Disease Mutation: The Sensitivity and Specificity of Measuring CAG Repeats." *New England Journal of Medicine* 330 (1994): 1401–1406.

Lanska, Douglas J. "George Huntington (1850–1916) and Hereditary Chorea." *Journal of the History of the Neurosciences* 9 (2000): 76–89.

Leder, Philip, and Marshall Nirenberg. "RNA Codewords and Protein Synthesis, II. Nucleotide Sequence of a Valine RNA Codeword." *Proceedings of the National Academy of Sciences of the United States of America* 52 (1964): 420–427.

————. "RNA Codewords and Protein Synthesis, III. On the Nucleotide Sequence of a Cysteine and a Leucine RNA Codeword." *Proceedings of the National Academy of Sciences of the United States of America* 52 (1964): 1521–1529.

Leeflang, Esther P., Simon Tavare, Paul Marjoram, Carolyn O. Neal, Jayalakshmi Srinidhi, Heather MacFarlane, Marcy E. MacDonald, et al. "Analysis of Germline Mutation Spectra at the Huntington's Disease Locus Supports a Mitotic Mutation Mechanism." *Human Molecular Genetics* 8 (1999): 173–183.

Leung, C.M., Y.W. Chan, C.M. Chang, Y.L. Yu, and C.N. Chen. "Huntington's Disease in Chinese: A Hypothesis of Its Origin." *Journal of Neurology, Neurosurgery, and Psychiatry* 55 (1992): 681–684.

Loening, U.E. "The Fractionation of High-molecular-weight Ribonucleic Acid by Polyacrylamide-gel Electrophoresis." *Biochemical Journal* 102 (1967): 251–257.

Luria, S.E., and M.L. Human. "A Nonhereditary, Host-induced Variation of Bacterial Viruses." *Journal of Bacteriology* 64 (1952): 557–569.

MacDonald, Marcy E., and James F. Gusella. "Huntington's Disease: Translating a CAG Repeat Into a Pathogenic Mechanism." *Current Opinion in Neurobiology* 6 (1996): 638–643.

Maddox, Brenda. *Rosalind Franklin: The Dark Lady of DNA*. New York: HarperCollins, 2002.

Meiser, Bettina, and Stewart Dunn. "Psychological Impact of Genetic Testing for Huntington's Disease: An Update of the

Literature." *Journal of Neurology, Neurosurgery & Psychiatry* 69 (2000): 574–578.

Mendel, Gregor. "Versuche über Plflanzenhybriden." *Verhandlungen des naturforschenden Vereines in Brünn, Bd. IV für das Jahr 1865. Abhandlungen* (1866): 3–47. Trans. William Bateson, with revisions and corrections by Roger Blumberg.

Mullis, Kary B., and Fred A. Faloona. "Specific Synthesis of DNA in Vitro via a Polymerase-catalyzed Chain Reaction." *Methods in Enzymology* 155 (1987): 335–350.

Nance, Martha A., and Richard H. Myers. "Juvenile Onset Huntington's Disease—Clinical and Research Perspectives." *Mental Retardation and Developmental Disabilities Research Reviews* 7 (2001): 153–157.

National Institute of Neurological Disorders and Stroke. *Huntington's Disease: Hope Through Research.* Rockville, Md.: National Institute of Neurological Disorders and Stroke, 2008. Available online. URL: http://www.ninds.nih.gov/disorders/huntington/detail_huntington.htm.

Nirenberg, Marshall, and Philip Leder. "RNA Codewords and Protein Synthesis: The Effect of Trinucleotides Upon the Binding of sRNA to Ribosomes." *Science* 145 (1964): 1399–1407.

Nirenberg, Marshall W., and J. Heinrich Matthaei. "The Dependence of Cell-free Protein Synthesis in E. Coli Upon Naturally Occurring or Synthetic Polyribonucleotides." *Proceedings of the National Academy of Sciences of the United States of America* 47 (1961): 1588–1602.

Okun, Michael S. "Huntington's Disease: What We Learned from the Original Essay." *Neurologist* 9 (2003): 175–179.

Okun, Michael S., and Nia Thommi. "Americo Negrette (1924 to 2003): Diagnosing Huntington's Disease in Venezuela." *Neurology* 63 (2004): 340–343.

Ørbeck, Alf L. "An Early Description of Huntington's Chorea." *Medical History* 3 (1959): 165–168.

Orr, Harry T., and Huda Y. Zoghbi. "Trinucleotide Repeat Disorders." *Annual Review of Neuroscience* 30 (2007): 575–621.

Osler, William. *On Chorea and Choreiform Affectations*. London: H.K. Lewis, 1894.

———. "Historical Note on Hereditary Chorea." *Neurographs* 1 (1908): 113–116.

Pearce, J.M.S. "Thomas Sydenham and Richard Bright on Chorea." *Journal of Neurology, Neurosurgery & Psychiatry* 58 (1995): 319.

Penney, John B. Jr., and Anne B. Young. "Striatal Inhomogeneities and Basal Ganglia Function." *Movement Disorders* 1 (1986): 3–15.

Reik, Wolf. "Genomic Imprinting: A Possible Mechanism for the Parental Origin Effect in Huntington's Chorea." *Journal of Medical Genetics* 25 (1988): 805–808.

Rice, Edward. *Captain Sir Richard Francis Burton: The Secret Agent Who Made the Pilgrimage to Mecca, Discovered the Kama Sutra, and Brought the* Arabian Nights *to the West*. New York: Charles Scribner's Sons, 1990.

Ridley, R.M., C.D. Frith, L.A. Farrer, and P.M. Conneally. "Patterns of Inheritance of the Symptoms of Huntington's Disease Suggestive of an Effect of Genomic Imprinting." *Journal of Medical Genetics* 28 (1991): 224–231.

Roberts, Richard J. "How Restriction Enzymes Became the Workhorses of Molecular Biology." *Proceedings of the National Academy of Sciences of the United States of America* 102 (2005): 5905–5908.

Robitaille, Yves, Iscia Lopes-Cendes, Mark Becher, Guy Rouleau, and Arthur W. Clark. "The Neuropathology of CAG

Repeat Diseases: Review and Update of Genetic and Molecular Features." *Brain Pathology* 7 (1997): 901–926.

Rosas, H.D., W.J. Koroshetz, Y.I. Chen, C. Skeuse, M. Vangel, M.E. Cudkowicz, K. Caplan, et al. "Evidence for More Widespread Cerebral Pathology in Early HD: An MRI-based Morphometric Analysis." *Neurology* 60 (2003): 1615–1620.

Ruddle, F.H., V.M. Chapman, T.R. Chen, and R.J. Klebe. "Genetic Analysis with Man-Mouse Somatic Cell Hybrids: Linkage Between Human Lactate Dehydrogenase A and B and Peptidase B." *Nature* 227 (1970): 251–257.

Sadri-Vakili, Ghazaleh, and Jang-Ho J. Cha. "Mechanisms of Disease: Histone Modifications in Huntington's Disease." *Nature Clinical Practice Neurology* 2 (2006): 330–338.

Saiki, Randall K., David H. Gelfand, Susanne Stoffel, Stephen J. Scharf, Russell Higuchi, Glenn T. Horn, Kary B. Mullis, et al. "Primer-directed Enzymatic Amplification of DNA with a Thermostable DNA Polymerase." *Science* 239 (1988): 487–491.

Saiki, Randall K., Stephen Scharf, Fred Faloona, Kary B. Mullis, Glenn T. Horn, Henry A. Erlich, and Norman Arnheim. "Enzymatic Amplification of β-globin Genomic Sequences and Restriction Site Analysis for Diagnosis of Sickle Cell Anemia." *Science* 230 (1985): 1350–1354.

Santachiara, A. Silvana, M. Nabholz, V. Miggiano, A.J. Darlington, and W. Bodmer. "Genetic Analysis with Man-Mouse Somatic Cell Hybrids: Linkage Between Human Lactate Dehydrogenase B and Peptidase B Genes." *Nature* 227 (1970): 248–251.

Schon, Eric A., and Giovanni Manfredi. "Neuronal Degeneration and Mitochondrial Dysfunction." *Journal of Clinical Investigation* 111 (2003): 313–312.

Sharp, Alan H., and Christopher A. Ross. "Neurobiology of Huntington's Disease." *Neurobiology of Disease* 3 (1996): 3–15

Smith, Hamilton O., and K.W. Wilcox. "A Restriction Enzyme from *Hemophilus Influenzae*: I. Purification and General Properties." *Journal of Molecular Biology* 51 (1970): 379–391.

Snell, Russell G., John C. MacMillan, Jeremy P. Cheadle, Iain Fenton, Lazarus P. Lazarou, Peter Davies, Marcy E. MacDonald, et al. "Relationship Between Trinucleotide Repeat Expansion and Phenotypic Variation in Huntington's Disease." *Nature Genetics* 4 (1993): 393–397.

Southern, E.M. "Detection of Specific Sequences Among DNA Fragments Separated by Gel Electrophoresis." *Journal of Molecular Biology* 98 (1975): 503–517.

Suffolk Gazette, "Sag Harbor." June 30, 1806.

Sydenham, Thomas. *The Works of Thomas Sydenham, M.D.* Translated from the Latin edition of Dr. Greenhill with a Life of the Author by Robert Gordon Latham. London: Sydenham Society, 1850.

Thomas, Madhavi, Tetsuo Ashizawa, and Joseph Jankovic. "Minocycline in Huntington's Disease: A Pilot Study." *Movement Disorders* 19 (2004): 692–695.

Tibben, Aad. "Predictive Testing for Huntington's Disease." *Brain Research Bulletin* 72 (2007): 165–171.

Tilney, Frederick. "A Family in Which the Choreic Strain May Be Traced Back to Colonial Connecticut." *Neurographs* 1 (1908): 125–127.

Tortora, Gerard J., and Sandra Reynolds Grabowski. *Principles of Anatomy and Physiology*, 10th ed. New York: John Wiley & Sons, 2003.

Walker, Francis O. "Huntington's Disease." *The Lancet* 369 (2007): 218–228.

Watson, J.D. *The Double Helix: A Personal Account of the Discovery of the Structure of DNA*. New York: Atheneum, 1968.

Watson, J.D., and F.H.C. Crick. "Molecular Structure of Nucleic Acids: A Structure for Deoxyribose Nucleic Acid." *Nature* 171 (1953): 737–738.

Weismann, August. *The Germ-plasm: A Theory of Heredity.* Translated by W. Newton Parker and Harriet Rönnefeldt. New York: Charles Scribner's Sons, 1893.

Wexler, Alice R. "Chorea and Community in a Nineteenth-century Town." *Bulletin of the History of Medicine* 76 (2002): 495–527.

———. *The Woman Who Walked Into the Sea: Huntington's and the Making of a Genetic Disease.* New Haven, Conn.: Yale University Press, 2008.

Wexler, N.S., E.A. Rose, and D.E. Housman. "Molecular Approaches to Hereditary Diseases of the Nervous System: Huntington's Disease as a Paradigm." *Annual Review of Neuroscience* 14 (1991): 503–529.

Wilkins, M.H.F., A.R. Stokes, and H.R. Wilson. "Molecular Structure of Nucleic Acids: Molecular Structure of Deoxypentose Nucleic Acids." *Nature* 171 (1953): 738–740.

Wood, H.C. *Nervous Diseases and Their Diagnosis: A Treatise Upon the Phenomena Produced by Diseases of the Nervous System, with Especial Reference to the Recognition of Their Causes.* Philadelphia: J.B. Lippincott Company, 1887.

The Woody Guthrie Foundation. *Woody Guthrie Biography.* New York: The Woody Guthrie Foundation and Archives, 2008. Available online. URL: http://www.woodyguthrie.org/biography/biography1.htm.

Yoon, Song-Ro, Louis Dubeau, Margot de Young, Nancy S. Wexler, and Norman Arnheim. "Huntington Disease Expansion Mutations in Humans Can Occur Before Meiosis Is Completed." *Proceedings of the National Academy of Sciences of the United States of America* 100 (2003): 8834–8838.

Young, Anne B. "Huntington's in Health and Disease." *Journal of Clinical Investigation* 111 (2003): 299–302.

FURTHER READING

Cray, Ed. *Ramblin' Man: The Life and Times of Woody Guthrie.* New York: W.W. Norton, 2004.

Glimm, Adele. *Gene Hunter: The Story of Neuropsychologist Nancy Wexler.* Washington, DC: Joseph Henry Press, 2005.

Karlen, Richard R. *Devil's Dance.* Scotch Plains, N.J.: Ironbound Press, 2008.

Klein, Joe. *Woody Guthrie: A Life.* New York: Dell, 1999.

Quarrel, Oliver W.J. *Huntington's Disease (The Facts).* New York: Oxford University Press, 2008.

Sulaiman, Sandy. *Learning to Live with Huntington's Disease: One Family's Story.* Philadelphia : Jessica Kingsley Publishers, 2007.

Wexler, Alice R. *Mapping Fate: A Memoir of Family, Risk, and Genetic Research.* New York: Random House, 1995.

————. *The Woman Who Walked Into the Sea: Huntington's and the Making of a Genetic Disease.* New Haven, Conn.: Yale University Press, 2008.

WEB SITES

The HD Lighthouse
http://hdlighthouse.org/
The goal of the HD Lighthouse is to provide up-to-date information on Huntington's disease research.

Hereditary Disease Foundation

http://www.hdfoundation.org/

The Hereditary Disease Foundation (HDF), which was founded by Nancy Wexler's father, Dr. Milton Wexler, provides political and financial support to biomedical research aimed toward finding cures for Huntington's disease and other hereditary diseases.

Huntington's Disease Advocacy Center

http://www.hdac.org/

This site grew out of a Huntington's disease-related listserv and a Huntington's disease-support group based at Massachusetts General Hospital. Its goal is to be a clearinghouse for information on Huntington's disease.

Huntington's Disease Society of America

http://www.hdsa.org/

The Huntington's Disease Society of America (HDSA) supports medical research about Huntington's disease, provides aid to those who suffer from Huntington's disease, and educates the public and health practitioners about the disease.

The Mayo Clinic: Huntington's Disease

http://www.mayoclinic.com/health/huntingtons-disease/DS00401

This page offers an informative summary of what is known about Huntington's disease, its diagnosis, and treatment.

Medline Plus: Huntington's Disease

http://www.nlm.nih.gov/medlineplus/huntingtonsdisease.html

Medline Plus is part of the National Library of Medicine. The Huntington's disease page offers a variety of information for those who wish to learn more about the disease.

National Institute for Neurological Diseases and Stroke: Huntington's Disease Information Page
http://www.ninds.nih.gov/disorders/huntington/huntington.htm
The National Institute for Neurological Diseases and Stroke is the arm of the National Institutes of Health that focuses on neurological diseases such as Huntington's disease.

PICTURE CREDITS

INDEX

ABOUT THE AUTHOR

David M. Lawrence has never decided what he will do when (if) he grows up. He is a scientist who has taught geography, meteorology, oceanography, and biology at the college level and who enjoys research in mountains, deserts, and plains as well as underwater. He is an author (*Upheaval from the Abyss: Ocean Floor Mapping and the Earth Science Revolution*) and award-winning journalist who covers everything from high school sports to international research in science and medicine. He is also a scuba diver looking for a way to make a living on the water. When not consumed with those activities, he looks at his guitars and wonders if he is too old to become a rock god. (It would help if he could actually play.) He lives in Mechanicsville, Virginia, with his wife, two children, and a menagerie of creatures with different combinations of legs, scales, and fins.